MW01002075

The People's Guide to the United States Constitution

THE PEOPLE'S GUIDE

GUIDE

TO THE
UNITED STATES
CONSTITUTION

Dave Kluge

**AMERICAN
HANDBOOK
PUBLISHING**

*Download your free Educator's Guide or Homeschool/
Self-Study Guide for this book at* **understandtheconstitution.com**

*Dedicated to Thomas Jefferson,
author of the Declaration of Independence*

This is an updated edition.

First edition hardcover published in 1994 by Carol Publishing Group

Second updated edition paperback published in 1996 by Carol Publishing Group

Third updated and expanded edition paperback published in 2008 by
Action Publishing

With special thanks to Ethel Yake Metzler for helping
to make this a better, easier-to-read book.

Cover illustration by Peter Green
Interior illustrations by Allen Harris
Typography by Lea Frechette

ISBN 978-0-9832152-0-2 (paperback)
ISBN 978-0-9832152-2-6 (hardback)
ISBN 978-0-9832152-1-9 (ebook)

Library of Congress Control Number: 2011916617

Manufactured in the United States of America
10 9 8 7 6 5 4 3

American Handbook Publishing
PO Box 29044
Los Angeles, CA 90029

Visit us online at **understandtheconstitution.com**

Table of Contents

Introduction

This book began with a realization that I did not know enough about our Constitution.

While watching a presidential campaign debate, I listened to each of the three leading candidates mention the Constitution in ways that seemed contradictory. Were any of their interpretations correct? I didn't know. In fact, I had to admit that I was among that large group of Americans who have not read our Constitution—or had not read it recently—and felt unfamiliar with its meanings. Thus I began my research.

Webster defines "constitution" as an agreement that sets in place a system of fundamental principles for the government of rational and social beings. A constitution, you might say, lays out the basic rules of the game for people who want freedom for themselves and for others.

Written to guarantee the rights of individuals and provide a framework for cooperation, the United States Constitution protects those rights. The result has been, in many ways, the most successful and prosperous society in history.

But what might happen if the players forget the rules of the game? Chaos, arguments, people making up their own rules. If we do not understand what the Constitution actually says, we could give up our rights and not even know it.

So this book was written for people, like me, who want to guarantee their own freedom and enjoy the benefits of living in a society, maybe even a world, which respects and protects human rights and freedom for all.

I hope that this book, the result of my own citizen self-education, will help give readers a basic understanding of what the Constitution actually says and, with this understanding, enable them to better decide for themselves how to claim and exercise their rights.

A recent survey asked, "What would it be like to live in a country where everyone you met had read and understood the Constitution?" People of all ages and groups said there would be more respect and cooperation, the government would not violate people's rights and people could work together to make that country better.

I'd like that. The Constitution and the human rights it protects provide a common ground we can all share. The power to protect and preserve our freedoms begins when "We the people" become familiar with our own Constitution.

We the People

On July 4, 1776, the representatives of the thirteen American Colonies dissolved all political connection to Great Britain and declared themselves free and independent. In support of the Declaration of Independence the signers pledged to each other "our lives, our fortunes and our sacred honor." In fact, if caught by the British after signing their names, these men surely would have been executed.

Freedom of speech and of assembly; 1st Amendment.

For twelve years that pledge was tested both in war and in the signers' commitment to create a system for our country that would preserve the rights and freedoms for which they fought. Such a system was devised and implemented when the United States Constitution was written in 1787.

The American form of government has been the most successful among nations for the last 230 years. The Constitution has been a beacon to all people seeking freedom in their own countries. Yet, how many of us today are truly familiar with the document and principles that we rely upon to guarantee our rights and freedoms?

For most people throughout history, the ideals expressed in the Declaration of Independence and the Constitution simply didn't exist. Not until the Golden Age of Greece (479 B.C. to 431 B.C.) did the idea of democracy—meaning government or rule by the people—begin to replace the practice of rule by kings and tyrants. Pericles, the most famous political leader of Athens, promoted the principle that the people had the right to know about their government, to voice their opinions concerning it and contribute to and participate in the political and economic activities of their culture.

The arts, freedom and prosperity of Athens achieved their highest expression during that period. The Greek ideas of individual rights and democratic freedom shaped the world and have been raised again and again to defeat tyrants and dictators.

The people who fought in the Revolutionary War and wrote the Constitution were well educated in the ideas of the Golden Age of Greece and the history of governments. They used these ideas in the Constitution.

Today, it becomes our responsibility to educate ourselves in the Constitution, to ask others to do the same, and to stand together on the common ground of our Constitution to protect our rights. The first duty of citizens is to tell the government what they want it to do.

No society or government has been perfect. The Greeks held slaves even during their Golden Age. History reveals numerous—some might say endless—examples of society's failure to live up to the ideals of human rights. But after the ideas of democracy and freedom had taken root in Greece, the playwright Euripides could stand up and speak out against slavery by declaring that it was "That thing of evil, by its nature evil, forcing submission from a man to what no man should yield to."

> "Just because you do not take an interest in politics doesn't mean politics won't take an interest in you."
>
> Pericles,
> Greek statesman,
> 495-429 B.C.

In a free society, the powers of government are given to the government by the people. By guaranteeing the right to speak freely and to influence the actions of their government—among the many rights guaranteed by the Constitution—the Constitution protects the ability of people to improve life for themselves, their families, their society and to remain free.

Before the Constitution became the highest law of the United States, fierce arguments were fought in newspapers, speeches, letters and pamphlets regarding what the Constitution should say. The individuals who wrote the Declaration of Independence and the Constitution were very well educated and made conscientious efforts to communicate exactly what they meant.

Therefore, it is important to grasp the original purpose for which these documents were written and to explore their meanings. While thousands of volumes of historical and legal analyses have been written about these documents, we can start with the originals, a few key words and some good dictionaries. Noah Webster's 1828 dictionary—the first great American dictionary—can give us important help since some of the concepts explained there have been lost to modern dictionaries.

Life, Liberty and the Pursuit of Happiness

The phrase "life, liberty and the pursuit of happiness" is at the heart of the Declaration of Independence. These words express the hopes of all people. The author of the Declaration of Independence recognized that these rights, so much a part of the basic nature of people, cannot be separated from them.

A right can be defined as a power or privilege which correctly belongs to one by law, nature or tradition. The American colonists felt that the King of Great Britain ignored their rights to life, liberty and the pursuit of happiness. They believed that government needed to secure those rights—not to deny them. Our study of the Declaration of Independence can lead the way to reading the Constitution.

The first right, "life," Webster broadly defines as the condition in which a plant's, an animal's or a human being's natural functions and motions are performed. In humankind, that state of being in which the spirit, intellect and body are united we identify as life. The source of the word "life" goes back to a meaning of "to be." So when we say "life" we are speaking about our right to be and to regulate or conduct our own existence.

The second of these basic rights "liberty," holds a meaning similar to "free" [able to think or act without restriction; independent]. When you have liberty you are free from arbitrary [not based on a known reason or rule; at the whim of someone else, such as a tyrant] control. Liberty also means release or freedom from slavery, imprisonment or other arbitrary restrictions. It comes from a root word meaning "belonging to the people, free" and also "to grow up, rise."

Looking more deeply at the word "liberty" we find two definitions that expand its meaning.

"Natural liberty," or the power to act as one thinks fit without any restraint or control except from the laws of nature, can be illustrated by this example. Here on Earth we cannot jump sixty feet into the air because of gravity, but we have the liberty to jump a foot or more, depending on our physical ability.

We can act as we individually see fit when we are by ourselves with no one else around. But what if we wish to live in the companionship of others, such as in a town or city? Then the term "civil liberty" comes into play.

"Civil" means relating to a person as a member of a community. It comes from a Latin word meaning "city."

"Civil liberty" is the liberty of persons in a society. Society restrains "natural liberty" for the safety of its citizens. So "liberty" in a civilized society has as part of its definition the control of the individual to the extent that the individual may not harm or hinder the liberty of another individual. Unnecessary restraint of natural liberty when an individual's actions do not threaten the public good is oppression and therefore not "liberty."

> "They that can give up essential liberty to obtain a little temporary safety deserve neither liberty nor safety."
> Benjamin Franklin, 1759

With liberty, people know what their rights are and that their rights will be respected.

Civil liberties, secured by establishing sensible guidelines or laws, protect both the individual and the common good. The Constitution does this, as do other laws based on the Constitution.

"Happiness" is that agreeable state of being in which desires are gratified; the enjoyment of pleasure without pain; good fortune. It comes from a root meaning "chance" and "good fortune." So the right to the "pursuit [from the Latin 'follow forward'] of happiness" contains the idea that you are free to follow a path that leads to good fortune—whatever that goal may be for you.

The Purpose of Government

The Declaration of Independence gives us the basic purpose of governments. It is, simply put, to secure the people's rights to "life, liberty and the pursuit of happiness."

To "govern" means to direct or control the actions and conduct of society, either by established laws or by the will of the ruler. Govern comes from a Latin word meaning to pilot a ship, direct or guide. As we shall see later, the first paragraph of the United States Constitution tells us the purpose of our government and the condition toward which we should be guided.

"Government" refers to both the system of rules and principles which guide a country and the administration of public affairs according to those rules and principles. The duties and powers of the people, representatives and institutions that administer those rules are defined and limited by law.

A "free country" is not dependent upon or controlled by another nation. A "free people" are subject only to fixed laws, made by the consent of the people, and fairly and consistently administered. So having a constitution in a free country such as the United States means that the people agree, consent to and choose how they are to be governed.

Our Constitution, the basis of this nation's freedom, continues to beckon to those less fortunate around the world. It lays out our fundamental laws, establishes the form of government, and defines the rights and liberties of all citizens. It stands above all other laws of our land.

A "constitution" is a system of fundamental rules, principles and laws that establishes the form of government in a state or country. In free countries, the constitution is above and more powerful than the laws of the country, as the constitution creates, defines, limits and controls the making of laws. Laws are the rules which direct and control both the people and those working in the government. The President of the United States, members of Congress and other government officials take oaths to "preserve, protect and defend" the Constitution. The word comes from "constitute," which means to fix or establish. So, our Constitution fixes or establishes our government's character and what it does.

The writers of the Constitution set up a republic. This form of government means supreme power rests with all the people entitled to vote and their elected representatives.

The word "democracy" refers to a government run directly by the people. "Demos," a Greek word for the people, combined with "cracy," derived from another Greek word meaning to rule, form the word democracy. A small town could have a democracy where each person voted on all matters concerning the small town; but with millions of people in the United States, it was considered much more practical to have a "republican" form of government where the people vote for representatives who then vote on their behalf. So, in the United States the people elect individuals to represent them. Then these "representatives" vote on matters of law and government. If the people don't like what their representatives do or how they vote, they elect other individuals to represent them.

> **The President makes a promise that he or she will, "faithfully execute the office of President of the United States, and will to the best of my ability, preserve, protect and defend the Constitution of the United States."** Representatives, senators and other government officials make a similar promise to uphold the Constitution.

The American government, based upon this Constitution, is the oldest, continuously existing governmental form in a major nation in the world today. All other major nations have undergone significant changes in their forms of government since the American Revolution of 1776. In Great Britain, for example, royalty, although still in existence, no longer has the same power it once held.

Our Founding Fathers brought the principles from the Age of Pericles, which was 2200 years earlier, to our government, making freedom of speech, the right to voice opinions and to participate in government essential parts of our system. Because of these principles, ancient Athens flourished in the time of Pericles, just as our United States has flourished since our Constitution was written and adapted.

We, a free people, created our government. It began with the consent and choice of the people and continues with their consent today. Our rights and privileges, fixed by laws and principles, help us maintain and keep our government operating as we voice our collective choices and consent by our actions such as voting or not voting, voicing our opinions or not voicing them, the way we spend our money and in fact, the way we live our lives.

The creators of the Declaration of Independence and the Constitution drafted these documents so that Americans could live better lives and flourish under a government based on liberty. These documents, written in turbulent times, became the key guides in forming the United States of America and in preserving it to this day.

Ideas and Events Leading to American Independence

The King of Great Britain at the time of the American Revolution derived his power from the "divine right of kings," a concept that alleges a king or queen rules by the will of God, not the will of the people. Thus, a king or queen could do no wrong. The divine right of kings differs greatly from the concepts of democracy and republic.

Pericles, 495-429 B.C.

Groups, governments and societies are always made up of individual people. Under the United States Constitution, the American people, as individuals, have unalienable [not capable of being sold, separated or transferred to another] rights. The Constitution explicitly explains these rights. The individuals in the United States at the time the Constitution was written consented and agreed to a democratic form of government whose Constitution established ways to preserve individual rights and the democratic form of government.

Greek Democracy

Although most forms of government over the past many thousands of years were kingdoms, where kings or queens ruled, there were forms of republics in ancient India as far back as the sixth century B.C. In the fifth century B.C., the city of Athens, in what is now Greece, had democratic forms of government.

Athens and other Greek "city-states" [an independent city that rules itself and its surrounding territory like a country] stressed the idea of rule by law and held that dictatorships were the worst form of government. During the Golden Age of Athens, each male citizen, whether commoner or noble, served equally in the body that passed all the laws and made important governmental decisions. However, neither slaves, who made up a large part of the population, nor women had the right to vote.

Democracy in ancient Athens came to an end around 404 B.C. after a war with the Greek city-state of Sparta. The ancient Romans also had forms of democracy that gave way to the dictatorships of the Roman Emperors.

Anglo-Saxons

The Anglo-Saxons, German tribes who settled in England starting in the fifth century, brought with them a tradition of government where the people had rights. Laws had to be approved by the people, the kings were elected and did not pass their position or kingdom on to their children. They had a parliament [a group of people who make the laws for a country], held trials by juries, considered property rights sacred, and people were required to honor the rights of others. As the centuries moved on, the Anglo-Saxon traditions began to erode, but these rights became part of English heritage and tradition.

John Locke

Although Locke died in 1704, well before the American Revolution, Locke's book *Two Treatises of Government* [a treatise is a written work dealing formally and systematically with a subject] published in 1690 had a great impact on America's War of Independence from Great Britain. Locke believed that Man had rights that included liberty, political equality, life, and property ownership. He wrote that the protection of Man's rights was the job of government and that a government justified its existence by protecting human rights better than men could.

Other of Locke's ideas that we can see in the Declaration of Independence include the concepts: 1) that people have the right to obtain a new government or rulers if their government or rulers do not protect their rights and 2) that the people should agree on how they should be ruled and who should rule them.

The American Colonies

England colonized the eastern coastal area of the United States north of Florida starting in 1607 with an English colony in what is now the State of Virginia. A colony is a group of people who settle in a place away from their native land, but remain under the political control of their native land. A colony can also refer to the land settled by these people. There were thirteen colonies with a total population of about two million people by 1776 when these colonies declared their independence from Great Britain.

The people living in these colonies were mainly British but also included other Europeans, Native American Indians, and slaves brought from Africa.

To the north of these American Colonies were French settlements in what is now Canada; to the south was the Spanish territory of Florida. Between 1689 and 1763 the British and French fought a number of wars, mainly due to conflicts in Europe, but conflicts also arose when both the British and French wanted to extend their territories in North America. In 1763 these wars ended with Britain gaining all of France's territory in North America east of the Mississippi River, excepting two tiny islands south of Newfoundland on the eastern part of what is now Canada. These two tiny islands remain French overseas territories. France's territory west of the Mississippi and the city of New Orleans went to Spain. But by 1800 Spain gave this territory back to France.

After the wars with the French ended in 1763, the British increased their control and taxation of the American colonies to strengthen their now enlarged American empire. Britain established a standing army in North America and made the colonists provide supplies and living quarters to these British troops. Britain passed laws restricting settlement in areas west of the Appalachian Mountains in order to maintain peaceful relations with the Indians in those areas. Also, new taxes were to be paid by the Americans so that the American Colonies could pay their share for keeping the British Empire. The colonists claimed Britain had no right to restrict their freedom or tax them because the colonists had no representation in the British government in England. "Taxation Without Representation is Tyranny" became a colonial slogan.

With tensions increasing between the Americans and British troops, Britain sent troops into New York City and Boston. In 1770, citizens of Boston angered with the presence of British troops in their city provoked the British troops to fire at them, killing several. This incident became known as the "Boston Massacre."

On December 16, 1773, American colonists dressed as Indians raided unguarded British ships in Boston Harbor and dumped chests full of tea into the water as a protest against British control and taxation. This incident, known as the "Boston Tea Party," has been recognized as a significant event leading to the war between the Colonies and Britain.

Common Sense by Thomas Paine

> "We fight not to enslave, but to set a country free, and to make room upon the earth for honest men to live in."
>
> Thomas Paine, 1777

Many of the people living in the original thirteen American Colonies were unhappy with the restrictions against moving into new territories to the west as well as paying new taxes and other burdens placed upon them by their British rulers. One such person was an Englishman named Thomas Paine, who had moved to the American Colonies in 1774. Paine's writing on religion and politics had a great impact on the American colonists and their leaders. On February 14, 1776, he published a pamphlet appropriately called *Common Sense*, which described life from the viewpoint of those American colonists who disliked the way they were governed by the British. *Common Sense* urged political freedom for the American Colonies from England and the creation of an American government. Both George Washington, America's military leader during the Revolutionary War and later the first president, and Thomas Jefferson, author of the Declaration of Independence and later the third president of the United States, agreed with Thomas Paine's *Common Sense*.

Paine told his readers that the independence of the American Colonies was to be a truly momentous event: "The cause of America is in great measure the cause of all mankind." Also, "We have it in our power to begin the world over again. A situation, similar to the present, hath not happened since the days of Noah until now. The birthday of a new world is at hand, and a race of men, perhaps as numerous as all Europe contains, are to receive their portion of freedom from the event of a few months."

Thomas Jefferson and the Declaration of Independence

On July 4, 1776, the thirteen Colonies declared their freedom from Great Britain and began calling themselves the United States of America, based upon a document called the Declaration of Independence. Thirty-three-year-old Thomas Jefferson wrote it.

Jefferson grew up on a farm in Virginia that he inherited at the age of fourteen when his father died. This enabled him to become an independent country gentleman. Thomas learned Latin, Greek, French, Spanish, Italian and Old English. He became familiar with higher mathematics and natural sciences. Jefferson, who had many American and foreign scholars among his friends, kept learning all his life. An expert violinist, he could sing and dance as well. He was also a good horseman. He became a lawyer and practiced law with great success before he started government work. Of course, he knew the history of democracy in ancient Athens. He knew that the rights to voice opinions and participate in government helped make Greek democracy a Golden Age. He understood the tradition of the Anglo-Saxons. He was also an excellent writer.

Jefferson, elected to the Virginia legislature in 1769, served there until 1775. A "legislature" is a group of elected people who have the power to make and cancel laws. Customarily, the persons who make up a legislature are elected by the people of the area where they live. These "legislators" represent the people that elected them.

Jefferson, along with others, was very active in the disagreements between the American Colonies and Britain. He and others protested taxes that Britain demanded the colonists pay. Feelings of protest in the Colonies rose to a point where the First Continental Congress was held in Philadelphia in 1774, two years before American independence. It was composed of fifty-six delegates chosen by and representing twelve of the Colonies. The colony of Georgia did not send delegates to the Congress; however

Georgia did agree to follow the plans made by the Congress. A "congress" in this use of the word means a meeting of individuals who will deal with matters for their common good.

Jefferson was sick and unable to attend this Congress, but he sent a written document setting forth his point of view. He stated that the British Parliament had no right to control the American Colonies. A parliament is a group of persons given the power and responsibility to make laws for a country or state. Jefferson argued that the first English people who had come to the American Colonies were in a situation similar to the Saxons and the Danes. The Saxons, who originally lived in an area of Germany, settled in Britain. Danes also settled in Britain from Denmark.

In July 1774, he presented his arguments in a widely circulated pamphlet titled *A Summary View of the Rights of British America*. Jefferson argued that the British Parliament had no more right to govern the American Colonies because they were settled by British people than the German or Danish governments had the right to rule over Britain just because people from Germany or Denmark had settled in Britain.

The Revolutionary War began April 19, 1775, when fighting broke out between American colonists and British soldiers at Lexington, Massachusetts. This forced the Second Continental Congress, convened in 1775, to organize the Colonies in their war against the British.

As the new government of the Colonies, this Congress approved an army and appointed George Washington commander in chief.

In 1775, the British Prime Minister proposed a peace plan prohibiting the British Parliament taxing the American colonists if the colonists would tax themselves. Jefferson, a leader of the Congress, wrote the reply to the British Prime Minister's plan. It was approved by the Congress. In this reply Jefferson made clear that a new American government had been set up for the American people, not Britain.

The Continental Congress asked Thomas Jefferson to draft a declaration of independence. Drawing upon the ideas of John Locke, Thomas Paine and others, Jefferson drafted a uniquely original and beautifully written document that stands as one of the most important in history. The Declaration of Independence elegantly stated the reasons why the American Colonies declared their freedom. It lists the grievances of the Colonies against British rule and declares the United States to be free and independent. The Congress adopted this declaration on July 4, 1776.

Thomas Jefferson, in his Declaration of Independence, lays out the purposes and goals of the United States—in essence, why the United States was formed. The Declaration of Independence has continued to inspire people from all over the world. We celebrate this date, July 4, as our

Independence Day, when we remember the thirteen Colonies formally declaring freedom from British rule and facing years of war with Britain.

Timeline of Events

1607: First English colony in North America started in what is now Virginia.

1690: John Locke published *Two Treatises of Government* in England. Locke taught that the duties of a government included the protection of liberty, life and property ownership of its citizens.

1689-1763: Wars between Britain and France. In 1763, Britain gained from France the territory of Canada. After this, Britain took many strong actions to control and tax the American Colonies.

December 16, 1773: "Boston Tea Party" took place. American colonists dressed as Indians dumped British tea into the ocean to protest British control and taxes.

July 1774: Thomas Jefferson wrote *A Summary View of the Rights of British America* arguing that Britain had no right to rule the American Colonies.

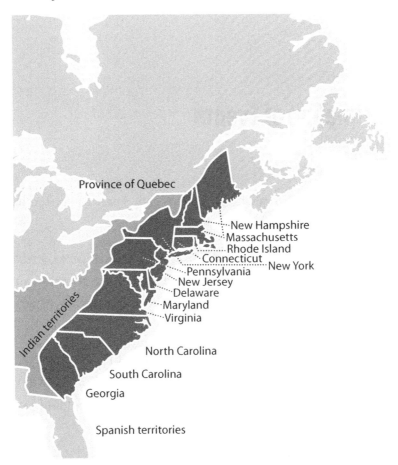

Province of Quebec

New Hampshire
Massachusetts
Rhode Island
Connecticut
New York
Pennsylvania
New Jersey
Delaware
Maryland
Virginia

Indian territories

North Carolina

South Carolina

Georgia

Spanish territories

September 5, 1774: First Continental Congress met in Philadelphia, Pennsylvania to protect the American Colonies against acts by the British Parliament.

April 19, 1775: Revolutionary War between the American Colonies and Britain started in Lexington, Massachusetts.

May 10, 1775: Second Continental Congress met in

Ireland

Great Britain
(Scotland, England & Wales)

France

Spain

Portugal

Continent of Africa

America and Europe at the time of the revolution

Philadelphia, and appointed George Washington commander in chief of the American army.

February 14, 1776: *Common Sense,* published by Thomas Paine, urged political freedom for the American Colonies from Great Britain.

July 4, 1776: The Second Continental Congress passed

the Declaration of Independence, written by Thomas Jefferson.

March 1, 1781: The Articles of Confederation, which were the basic laws of the United States before the Constitution became effective.

September 3, 1783: Final peace treaty signed between the United States and Great Britain.

May 25, 1787: Convention in Philadelphia began with the original purpose to revise the Articles of Confederation. Instead, the Constitution was drafted.

September 17, 1787: Delegates to the Philadelphia Convention signed the Constitution.

June 21, 1788: The Constitution was ratified [adopted] by the United States.

The Declaration of Independence

The complete text of The Declaration of Independence is presented here in **bold type**. Definitions of words and commentary are in regular type and enclosed by [square brackets] where they occur within a sentence of the original text. Spelling, capitalization, punctuation and paragraph styles have changed over the years, so modern styles are used for easier reading. The Declaration of Independence can be seen and read in its original wording without inserted definitions and commentary in the Appendix of this book.

IN CONGRESS, July 4, 1776.

The unanimous Declaration [a public announcement. Declaration comes from a Latin word meaning "make quite clear."] **of the thirteen United States of America,**

When in the course of human events, it becomes necessary for one people [the group of persons who make up a nation] **to dissolve the political** [relating to government] **bands** [things that bind or unite] **which have connected them with another, and to assume** [to take] **among the powers** [influential countries] **of the earth, the separate and equal station** [position or rank] **to which the Laws of Nature** [nature is the entire universe; or the creator of all things or the operation of the power that creates all things. The Laws of Nature include the idea of unchanging moral principles that form the basis for human conduct.] **and of Nature's God entitle them, a decent** [fit or suitable] **respect** [that positive view or honor in which we hold the good qualities of others] **to the opinions of mankind requires that they should declare the causes which impel** [drive or urge forward] **them to the separation.**

We hold these truths to be self-evident [producing certainty or clear conviction upon direct observation]**, that all men are created equal, that they are endowed** [provided with a quality or power] **by their Creator with certain unalienable** [not able to be given or taken away] **rights, that among these are life, liberty, and the pursuit of happiness.**

That to secure these rights, governments are instituted [established] **among men, deriving their just** [honest; conforming exactly to the laws and principles of right social conduct] **powers from the consent** [permission] **of the governed.**

That whenever any form of government becomes destructive of these ends [intended purposes], **it is the right of the people to alter or to abolish it, and to institute new government, laying its foundation on such principles and organizing its powers in such form, as to them shall seem most likely to effect** [produce or cause] **their safety and happiness. Prudence** [good judgment], **indeed, will dictate that govern-ments long established should not be changed for light and transient** [short duration; not lasting] **causes; and accordingly all experience has shown, that mankind are more disposed** [made willing; inclined] **to suffer, while evils are sufferable** [able to be tolerated], **than to right** [relieve from wrong] **themselves by abolishing the forms to which they are accustomed. But when a long train** [a series] **of abuses and usurpations** [wrongful or forceful takings of rights or powers], **pursuing invariably the same object,** [aim or goal] **evinces** [shows or indicates] **a design** [plan or purpose] **to reduce them under absolute despotism** [a tyranny; unjust and oppressive government], **it is their right, it is their duty** [that which a person owes to another; that which a person is bound by any natural or moral obligation to do or perform], **to throw off such govern-ment, and to provide new guards for their future security.**

Such has been the patient sufferance [tolerance; endurance such as of pain or misery] **of these Colonies; and such is now the necessity which constrains** [in this context, "constrains" means forces or compels] **them to alter their former systems of government. The history of the present King of Great Britain is a history of repeated injuries and usurpations, all having in direct object** [ultimate purpose] **the establishment of an absolute tyranny** [oppressive or unjust government] **over these States. To prove this, let facts be submitted to a candid** [free from prejudice, fair or impartial] **world.**

He has refused his assent [agreement or consent] **to laws, the most wholesome and necessary for the public good.**

After the Colonies passed laws, they had to be approved in Britain. The king rejected many such laws desired by the Colonies.

He has forbidden his governors to pass laws of immediate and pressing importance, unless suspended in their operation until his assent [consent; agreement] **should be obtained; and when so suspended, he has utterly neglected to attend to them.**

The governors of the Colonies were usually appointed

by the king and were not allowed to implement laws passed by the Colonies until the king approved them. The king sometimes took years to approve or reject them.

When people in the Colonies moved to new and unsettled land, the king and the British government disallowed new boundaries for legislative districts. This meant that these colonists would not be represented in their colonial legislatures. The next paragraph addresses these issues.

He has refused to pass other laws for the accommodation [the process of adapting or adjusting to someone or something] **of large districts of people, unless those people would relinquish the right of representation in the legislature,** [The American Colonies had their own legislatures even under British rule.] **a right inestimable** [too valuable or precious to be properly measured or estimated] **to them, and formidable** [in this context, "formidable" means feared or dreaded] **to tyrants only.**

He has called together legislative bodies at places unusual, uncomfortable, and distant from the depository [a place where anything is kept for safekeeping] **of their public records, for the sole purpose of fatiguing** [to weaken by harassing] **them into compliance with his measures.**

He has dissolved representative houses [Representative houses are legislatures. They are composed of representatives of the people who meet and make laws.] **repeatedly, for opposing with manly** [brave] **firmness his invasions on the rights of the people.**

The king's governors often dissolved colonial legislatures for passing laws the governors and the king did not agree with.

He has refused for a long time, after such dissolutions, to cause others to be elected; whereby the legislative powers, incapable of annihilation [being wiped out completely], **have returned to the people at large** [in general] **for their exercise** [performance of duties]; **the State remaining in the meantime exposed to all the dangers of invasion from without, and convulsions within.**

He has endeavored to prevent the population of these States; for that purpose obstructing the laws for naturalization [giving to a person of foreign birth the rights of citizenship in a new country] **of foreigners; refusing to pass others to encourage their migrations hither** [to this place], **and raising the conditions of new appropriations** [assigning for a particular use] **of lands.**

Many people wanted to settle in undeveloped areas farther west (or farther inland from the Atlantic Ocean).

The Colonies therefore wanted laws that made it easy for new settlers to buy land and become citizens. However, in 1763, the king claimed for himself these western lands and obstructed citizenship laws. In 1773, the king denied naturalization to foreigners. In 1774, he greatly increased the price of undeveloped land.

He has obstructed the administration of justice, by refusing his assent to laws for establishing judiciary [dealing with courts of law] **powers.**

The legislature of North Carolina wanted to set up a court system, but the king's government objected to part of what North Carolina wanted. So, this colony had no courts for years.

He has made judges dependent on his will alone, for the tenure [the duration, act, manner, or right of holding something] **of their offices, and the amount and payment of their salaries.**

The judges in the Colonies were paid by the king and served only so long as the king was pleased with their judgments. Obviously, if the judges were paid by the king and not the colonists, the judges would be more inclined to give judgments which the king would approve.

He has erected a multitude of new offices [duties

to be done under the authority of a government], **and sent hither swarms of officers** [people appointed to positions of responsibility in a government] **to harass our people, and eat out their substance** [means of living].

Great Britain started taxing various products shipped into the Colonies in 1767, and also sent numerous tax collectors to the American Colonies to collect these new taxes.

He has kept among us, in times of peace, standing [remaining permanently in existence] **armies, without the consent of our legislatures.**

Between 1754 and 1763, France and Great Britain fought a war in the American Colonies. The king kept his army in America after this war.

He has affected [In this context, "affected" means to seek to obtain; to aim at; aspire to.] **to render** [to cause to be; make] **the military independent of and superior to the civil** [relating to the community, or to the policy and government of the citizens] **power.**

The American government in Massachusetts was changed by the king's government and the British chief military commander in the American Colonies was named governor of Massachusetts.

He has combined with others to subject us to a jurisdiction [the power to make, declare or apply the law; or the power to govern] **foreign to our constitution** [the state of being; or the way a thing is composed or made up]**, and unacknowledged by our laws; giving his assent to their acts of pretended legislation:**

In 1766, a law was passed in Britain giving the king and the British Parliament the power to make laws for the Colonies, without the consent of the Colonies.

For quartering [lodging] **large bodies of armed troops among us;**

The Colonies were required to provide lodging and supplies to British troops in America.

For protecting them, by a mock [imitating reality but not real] **trial, from punishment for any murders which they should commit on the inhabitants of these States;**

British soldiers and British government representatives accused of murder while on duty in Massachusetts could be tried in Britain per a 1774 British law, shielding them from justice in the American Colonies.

For cutting off our trade with all parts of the world;

There were many British laws controlling American trade. American ships that did not comply with these laws could be taken by Great Britain.

For imposing taxes on us without our consent;

For depriving us, in many cases, of the benefits of trial by jury;

For transporting us beyond seas to be tried for pretended offenses;

A law passed by the British Parliament stated that colonists accused of treason could be tried in England.

For abolishing the free system of English laws in a neighboring province, ["a neighboring province" here refers to Quebec] **establishing therein an arbitrary** [absolute or unrestricted] **government, and enlarging its boundaries so as to render it at once an example and fit** [convenient] **instrument** [someone or something used as a means for accomplishing a specific purpose] **for introducing the same absolute rule into these Colonies;**

Britain had previously acquired the former French area of Quebec, which is now in Canada. In 1774, Britain passed a law providing for French civil law to be applied in Quebec, not English civil law. Britain also extended the territory of Quebec down into what is now Michigan, Wisconsin, Illinois, Ohio and Indiana.

For taking away our charters [a document which outlines the conditions under which a colony is organized], **abolishing our most valuable laws, and altering fundamentally the forms of our governments;**

A new British law drastically altered the charter and government of Massachusetts in 1774, and also restricted town meetings.

For suspending our own legislatures, and declaring themselves invested [provided with something] **with power to legislate for us in all cases whatsoever** [of any kind].

He has abdicated [gave up a right, responsibility or duty] **government** [the action of controlling or regulating a nation] **here, by declaring us out of his protection and waging war against us.**

The Revolutionary War began more than a year earlier.

He has plundered our seas, ravaged our coasts, burnt our towns, and destroyed the lives of our people.

The British navy seized American ships that violated

British law and used cannons against American seaports.

He is at this time transporting large armies of foreign mercenaries [hired soldiers] **to complete the works** [actions, deeds] **of death, desolation and tyranny, already begun with circumstances of cruelty and perfidy** [treachery] **scarcely paralleled** [equaled] **in the most barbarous ages, and totally unworthy of the head of a civilized nation.**

German mercenaries were used by the British to help fight the American colonists. Leaders of the Continental Congress and the American Army instructed that the war should be fought with respect for human rights. However, a campaign of atrocities against American soldiers and civilians was conducted by the king's army. British officers threatened their own soldiers and German mercenaries with severe punishment if they allowed mercy to American colonists who surrendered. Americans who were captured experienced torture, starvation and cruel maltreatment aboard British prison ships.

He has constrained our fellow citizens taken captive on the high seas to bear arms against their country, to become the executioners of their friends and brethren [people closely united or associated]**, or to fall themselves by their hands.**

Americans aboard American ships seized by the British were forced to join the British navy. Hence, Americans were forced by the British to kill other Americans or to be killed by Americans they were forced to fight.

He has excited [created] **domestic insurrections** [revolts] **amongst us, and has endeavored to bring on the inhabitants of our frontiers, the merciless Indian savages, whose known rule of warfare, is an undistinguished** [not making a distinction among or between] **destruction of all ages, sexes and conditions.**

In 1775, the British granted freedom to Virginia's slaves if they would help the British fight the colonists. The British also wanted to use American Indians to fight the colonists.

In every stage of these oppressions we have petitioned [made a formal request] **for redress** [the setting right of what is wrong; satisfaction or compensation for a wrong or injury] **in the most humble** [submissive] **terms: our repeated petitions have been answered only by repeated injury. A prince, whose character is thus marked by every act which may define a tyrant, is unfit to be the ruler of a free people.**

The Colonies petitioned the king to correct many British

abuses, but these petitions were ignored and followed by worse British abuses.

Nor have we been wanting [lacking] **in attentions to our British brethren. We have warned them from time to time of attempts by their legislature to extend an unwarrantable** [unjustified] **jurisdiction over us. We have reminded them of the circumstances of our emigration and settlement here. We have appealed** [made an urgent request] **to their native** [produced by nature; natural] **justice and magnanimity** [the quality of being noble and generous in one's conduct and rising above pettiness or meanness], **and we have conjured** [in this context, "conjured" means asked earnestly] **them by the ties of our common kindred** [relationship by blood] **to disavow** [repudiate or condemn] **these usurpations** [acts of seizing or occupying and enjoying the property of another, without right], **which, would inevitably** [unavoidably] **interrupt our connections and correspondence** [communication]. **They too have been deaf to the voice of justice and of consanguinity** [relationship by descent from the same ancestor; relationship by blood; kinship; close relationship]. **We must, therefore** [for that reason], **acquiesce** [agree without protest] **in the necessity, which denounces** [in this context, "denounces" means announces] **our separation, and hold them, as we hold the rest of mankind, enemies in war, in peace, friends.**

The Americans also appealed to the British people for justice through letters and pamphlets because of the common ancestry of most American colonists and the British people, but these appeals were also ignored.

We, therefore, the representatives of the United States of America, in general [relating to or including all members] **congress** [a meeting or assembly of delegates]**, assembled, appealing to the Supreme Judge of the world for the rectitude** [correctness of behavior] **of our intentions, do, in the name, and by authority of the good people of these Colonies, solemnly publish** [formally announce] **and declare** [to state that a person or thing exists in a certain way]**, that these united Colonies are, and of right** ["of right" as a result of having a moral or legal claim] **ought to be free and independent states; that they are absolved** [set free or released] **from all allegiance** [tie or obligation of a person to his king or government] **to the British Crown** [the power of a king]**, and that all political connection between them and the state of Great Britain, is and ought to be totally dissolved; and that as free and independent states, they have full power to levy war** ["levy war" means to make war]**, conclude** [to make a final determination] **peace, contract alliances, establish commerce, and to do all other acts and things which independent states may of right do.**

And for the support of this declaration, with a firm

reliance on the protection of divine Providence [God or the protective care of nature as a spiritual power]**, we mutually pledge to each other our lives, our fortunes and our sacred honor.**

The Continental Congress adopted the Declaration of Independence on July 4th 1776, and it was signed by the president of the Congress, John Hancock. Hancock is famous for his bold act of clearly signing his name to this document. Even today, when someone signs a document he is putting his "John Hancock" on it. It was later written on parchment in beautiful handwriting and signed by fifty-six members of the Congress. The original parchment copy is displayed at the National Archives in Washington, D.C.

The Declaration of Independence has been a beacon that has guided the hearts and minds of people ever since in their quests for governments to protect their freedom and rights to life, liberty and the pursuit of happiness. Indeed, many countries have found inspiration in our Declaration of Independence when their people demanded freedom from their own colonial masters. The Declaration of Independence shows who we are as a people.

Ideas and Events Leading to the Constitution

For the seven years following the Declaration of Independence, a war continued between the United States and Great Britain. A treaty of peace was signed on September 3, 1783. The United States had won its freedom.

At that time, the individual states largely governed themselves. They collected their own taxes; enforced their own laws; paid their own debts from the war; negotiated for themselves with foreign governments; dealt with Indian tribes; regulated trade between the states, and so on. There was no strong national government as we know it today.

A weak national government was set up to rule the thirteen independent states through a document called the Articles of Confederation. An article is a section or part of a written document such as a treaty, constitution or contract. A confederation is a group of independent nations or states joined together. The "Articles of Confederation" is the document that was the first "constitution" of the United States— it was replaced in its entirety by our present Constitution.

The Articles of Confederation allowed the states to remain independent— each state could do more or less as it pleased and did not have to obey the national government. This type of government was favored because the states had fought to end the unreasonable and harsh rule of Great Britain, and wanted to avoid an all-powerful national government which might have ruled them just as harshly and unreasonably as Britain had done.

However, this weaker national government proved unworkable. States printed their own paper money, which was not backed by gold or silver. It soon became worthless. Trade between the states slowed because the states taxed goods moving from one state to another. There was even an armed rebellion by farmers in Massachusetts in 1786 led by Daniel Shays. The Shays Rebellion protested high taxes and the severity of legal action against farmers who could not pay their debts.

Four years after the Revolutionary War, in 1787, delegates from twelve of the thirteen states met at a convention in Philadelphia to revise the Articles of Confederation. However, after this convention got underway, most of the delegates agreed to draw up a completely new system of government to replace the Articles of Confederation, instead of revising them. This convention proceeded to draft a constitution and create a national government that would be strong enough to rule the country and protect the people's and the states' individual rights as well.

Ideas differed within the states as to what powers the national government should have. These differences were worked out in compromises. Three of the main areas of compromise reached in drafting our Constitution were:

1. The larger states demanded representation based on their population, but smaller states demanded each state have the same representation. This was compromised by creating two separate bodies of representatives for the legislature, one based on population (the House of Representatives) and one based on being a state (the Senate). That way, the larger states had more representatives based on population in the House of Representatives and the smaller states had the same representation as the larger states in the Senate.

2. The states had different economic interests. The southern states were mainly agricultural and depended upon slave labor, while the northern ones were more heavily involved in manufacturing and commerce. A compromise was made where the national government:

   a. Could regulate commerce;

   b. Could not pass laws against bringing slaves into the country before 1808;

c. Could not tax goods being shipped out of the country;

d. Could make agreements with foreign countries but the agreements needed special approval by the state's representatives.

3. The northern states wanted to include within the Constitution a design that would end the slave trade. However, since representation in the House of Representatives was to be based on each state's population, allowing the Southern states to count their entire population would increase their representation, making any attempts by abolitionists within Congress to end slavery much more difficult.

The final compromise reached was that each slave would count as three-fifths of a person for both representation and tax purposes, which was similar to the arrangements under the existing Articles of Confederation. The South wanted the slave trade to continue indefinitely, but compromised that it would end within twenty years in exchange for prohibiting taxes on exports.

This issue of slavery in Colonial America and later the United States is a vast and grim subject. Prior to the Civil War, many Americans believed the Constitution was a pro-slavery document, including Frederick Douglass, a runaway slave who would later become perhaps the most famous African-American of the nineteenth century. Escaping from slavery in Baltimore, Maryland, in 1838, Douglass made his way to New York to find freedom. Because of his exceptional skills as an orator and original thinker, he became the leading advocate for abolition of slavery in the mid-to-late 1800s.

After a careful study of the Constitution, Douglass came to see our Founding Fathers' principles enshrined in the Declaration of Independence and the Constitution not as pro-slavery, but as strongly anti-slavery. He did not ignore that the Founding Fathers had failed to resolve the problem of slavery which had been introduced by the British much earlier, but he did recognize that while many Founding Fathers were themselves slave owners, many others were staunch and determined abolitionists. Most importantly, after his study of the Constitution, Douglass spoke and wrote of how each portion of the Constitution which refers to slavery actually condemned it. For example, he stated in 1860, "Therefore, instead of encouraging slavery, the Constitution encourages freedom by giving an increase of 'two-fifths' of political power to free [states] over slave States. So much for the three-fifths clause; taking it at its worst, it still leans to freedom, not slavery; for, be it remembered that the Constitution nowhere forbids a coloured man to vote."

Douglass felt the actual language of the Constitution meant that many of its writers intended for the eventual ending of slavery via legal avenues, but by 1860, he came to realize that slavery would need to be defeated by a civil war, which did begin a year later.

The system of national government that deals with matters that individual states have in common (even though the individual states have their own state governments) is called the "federal system." The federal government is also called the national government, the government of the United States, or the central government.

The word "federal" comes from a Latin word, which means "league." "League" means an agreement and alliance between states for their mutual aid and defense. "Federal" means a league of states that have agreed to cooperate with each other for a specific purpose or purposes. Hence, we have our federal government of the United States, which is the central or national government. This federal government is made from the agreement of the states to cooperate with each other.

A federal government system allows individual states to retain their own governments. The Constitution created our national government and laid out its powers and purposes.

Before the U.S. Constitution was written, several states had their own state constitutions which laid out how those state governments would operate.

The writers of the Constitution were well educated in the best and worst of governments from Greece, Rome, England, the American Colonies and elsewhere. Guided by the principle that the individual had a right to know about and participate in his government and the right to be protected by his government, they created a government controlled by the people where it was possible for rational and social beings to prosper.

George Washington, and others, greatly influenced the Constitution. As the man selected to preside over the convention, Washington's prestige, calming influence and guidance were significant factors in assisting the delegates to reach the many compromises necessary to balance all the competing interests.

James Madison has been called "the Father of the Constitution" because he devised the system of three branches of government — executive, legislative and judicial — which constitute the backbone of our form of government. Madison later became the fourth president of the United States and was a close friend of Thomas Jefferson.

The only full record of the debates and compromises at the Constitutional Convention is Madison's *Notes on the Federal Convention*. Madison's notes were extensively used in the actual writing of the Constitution.

Gouverneur Morris, a New York lawyer and head of the Convention committee charged with writing the final draft, physically penned the Constitution by putting the decisions reached by the members down on paper.

Thomas Jefferson stated on March 18, 1789, "The example of changing a constitution by assembling the wise men of the state, instead of assembling armies, will be worth as much to the world as the former examples we had give[n] them. The constitution, too, which was the result of our deliberation, is unquestionably the wisest ever yet presented to men."

After the Constitutional Convention reached agreement on the form of a new national government that was stronger than the previous government under the Articles of Confederation, the new Constitution had to be approved by nine states before it became law. Because this proposed stronger national government was to have powers previously exercised by the states, initially there was much opposition to the new Constitution.

Those persons who opposed the new Constitution giving the federal government these additional powers were called Anti-Federalists; those who approved of it were called Federalists. Newspapers at that time in 1787 were filled with many arguments for and against the new Constitution. Among the arguments against the proposed new government were:

– It would turn the individual states into one overall government;

– It might do away with the laws, customs and constitutions of the individual states;

– That the office of president was too powerful;

– That the rights of individual citizens were not clearly listed and spelled out in a "bill of rights" [A bill is a list of items. A bill of rights is a list of rights and freedoms a people have.];

– That it would increase taxes on land and other property;

– That the new federal government would become all-important to the detriment of individual citizens and states;

– That the Constitutional convention had exceeded its authority, since it was only supposed to propose amendments to the Articles of Confederation, not write a new constitution.

Opposition to the new Constitution was strongest in agricultural areas that mainly needed better roads and court services, which could be supplied by state and local governments, and so these people didn't feel a need for a stronger federal government.

Those favoring the new Constitution were mainly ship owners and traders near the Atlantic coast and frontiersmen who were inland from the Atlantic. They felt the United States needed a stronger national government to conduct foreign relations and military policies and put an end to trade barriers among the individual states.

In the many debates over the new Constitution, the feature that was most criticized was a lack of a bill of rights. Those favoring ratification promised to add a bill of rights by amending the Constitution, and with this promise enough support was gained to ratify the Constitution.

The Constitution was adopted in 1788. Since that time, the Constitution has been the supreme law of the United States.

Summary of the U.S. Constitution

The U.S. Constitution separates the powers of the federal government into three separate branches. This "separation of powers" was done to safeguard against tyranny as well as to prevent any one branch from becoming too powerful.

"Legislative" means having the power to make laws. The legislative branch makes the federal laws. Article I of the Constitution describes the legislative branch, called Congress.

Congress is divided into two "houses," the House of Representatives, whose members are called "representatives," and the Senate, whose members are called "senators."

The Senate and the House of Representatives occupy different sections of the same Capitol building in Washington, D.C. Each has its own large meeting room called the House Chamber and the Senate Chamber.

The "executive" branch of the federal government is responsible for carrying out the laws or overseeing their enforcement. This second branch of the federal government is described in Article II of the Constitution. The president heads the executive branch and lives in and has his office in the White House.

"Judicial" refers to judges, courts or their functions. A judge is a public official appointed to decide cases in a court of law. The Supreme Court heads the judicial or third branch of the federal government. Article III of the Constitution describes this branch. Nine judges, called "justices," sit on the Supreme

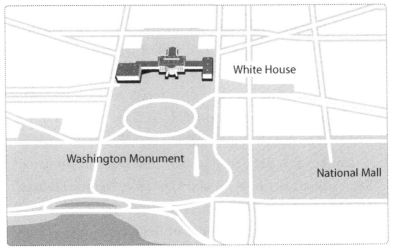

White House

Washington Monument

National Mall

Washington, D.C. became the capital of the United States in 1800. The legislative branch of government—both the House of Representatives and the Senate—is located in the United States Capitol Building

Court—one Chief Justice and eight Associate Justices.

The Constitution consists of seven major sections called "Articles." Below are brief descriptions of the seven Articles:

Article I establishes Congress as the body which makes

laws, and describes and limits its powers.

Article II establishes the office of the president as the office that executes the laws and limits its powers.

Article III establishes the Supreme Court and lower courts and their authority.

Article IV describes how states shall deal with each other, how new states may be admitted to the United States, and

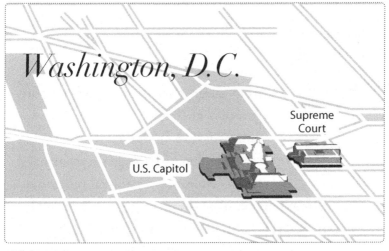

(capitol, spelled with an "o," is the name of the building itself). The executive branch is located in the White House, and the judicial branch in the Supreme Court Building.

guarantees that each state shall be protected by the federal government from invasion.

Article V describes how amendments may be added to the Constitution.

Article VI deals with debts owed by the United States prior to 1788, when the Constitution was adopted. This article also requires government officials to support the Constitution.

Article VII gives the steps to be followed for the adoption of the Constitution.

> Our Constitution is in actual operation; everything appears to promise that it will last; but in this world nothing is certain but death and taxes.
>
> Benjamin Franklin, 1789

The Constitution has been amended twenty-seven times. The first ten amendments, called the "Bill of Rights," protect people's freedom and liberty from unreasonable interference by the government. These ten amendments were ratified in 1791:

Amendment 1: Congress cannot make laws establishing a national religion or preferring one religion over another religion or prohibiting the free exercise of religion. It also cannot make laws reducing or restricting freedom of speech or the press, or limit the right of people to peaceably assemble and petition the government to correct wrongs.

Amendment 2: Gives the people the right to keep and bear arms.

Amendment 3: Prevents soldiers from being housed in private homes without the consent of the owners.

Amendment 4: Protects citizens against unreasonable searches and seizures.

Amendment 5: Sets the limits of criminal law. It also states that private property cannot be taken for public use without just compensation.

Amendment 6: States the rights of persons accused of crimes.

Amendment 7: Deals with civil suits and the right to have a trial by jury.

Amendment 8: Forbids excessive bail, excessive fines, and cruel and unusual punishment.

Amendment 9: Protects rights not laid out in the Constitution.

Amendment 10: Preserves for the states or the people any powers not given to the federal government.

The remaining seventeen amendments were ratified between 1798 and 1992:

Amendment 11: Limits the power of the courts. (Adopted in 1798)

Amendment 12: Describes how the president and the vice president are elected. (Adopted in 1804)

Amendment 13: Abolishes slavery. (Adopted in 1865)

Amendment 14: Deals with citizenship and other rights, as well as elections. It states that no person who has engaged in rebellion against the United States or given aid or comfort to enemies of the United States may hold any federal government office. It also deals with debt of the United States. (Adopted in 1868, after the Civil War)

Amendment 15: States that the right to vote may not be denied on account of race, color or having been a slave. (Adopted in 1870)

Amendment 16: Gives Congress the power to collect income taxes. (Adopted in 1913)

Amendment 17: Allows the people, not the state legislatures, to elect U.S. senators. (Adopted in 1913)

Amendment 18: Prohibits alcohol. (Adopted in 1919, but repealed by the Twenty-first Amendment)

Amendment 19: Gives women the right to vote. (Adopted in 1920)

Amendment 20: Sets the terms of the president and vice president; when Congress shall meet; and what should happen if the president elect dies before assuming office. (Adopted in 1933)

Amendment 21: Repeals the Eighteenth Amendment (prohibition of alcohol). (Adopted in 1933)

Amendment 22: Establishes how many terms the president may hold that office. (Adopted in 1951)

Amendment 23: Enables the people of Washington, D.C. to participate in the election of the president and vice president. (As Washington, D.C. is not a state, prior to this amendment citizens in Washington, D.C. could not participate in presidential elections.) (Adopted in 1961)

Amendment 24: The right of citizens to vote in presidential or congressional elections cannot be denied by failure to pay taxes. (Adopted in 1964)

Amendment 25: Deals with the removal of the president and what should occur if the office of the vice president is vacant. (Adopted in 1967)

Amendment 26: Gives 18-year-olds the right to vote. (Adopted in 1971)

Amendment 27: Bans midterm congressional pay raises. (Adopted in 1992)

The Constitution

The complete text of the Constitution is printed here in **bold type**. Definitions of words and commentary are in regular type and enclosed by [square brackets] where they occur within a sentence of the original text. Modern spelling, capitalization, punctuation and paragraph styles are used. The Constitution can be seen and read in its original wording without inserted definitions and a minimum of commentary in the Appendix of this book.

The first paragraph of the Constitution is called "The Preamble." A preamble is an introduction, especially an introduction to a constitution, law or legal document that states the purpose or intent of the document.

The purpose of the Constitution is eloquently stated in the Preamble to the United States Constitution. This purpose is the compass that guides our understanding as we study it.

We the People of the United States, in order to form **a more perfect Union** [a group of independent states joined together for some specific purpose], **establish justice** [behavior or treatment based on what is morally right or fair; or, the administration of the law or authority in maintaining this.], **insure domestic** [refers to one's own country] **tranquility** [calmness], **provide for the common defense, promote the general** [concerning all or most people] **welfare** [prosperity and happiness], **and secure the blessings** [benefits] **of liberty to ourselves and our posterity** [all of a person's descendants; all future generations or future mankind], **do ordain** [officially order] **and establish** [set up on a permanent basis] **this Constitution for the United States of America.**

Article I.

Section 1. All legislative powers herein [in this document] **granted shall be vested** [placed in the control of a person or group] **in a Congress** [a body of persons with the power to make laws] **of the United States, which shall consist of a Senate and House of Representatives.**

The next section describes the House of Representatives, composed of members who are elected to two-year terms. Eligible and qualified voters in the states elect members of the House of Representatives. The language of the Constitution describes qualified voters as those who are qualified to vote for members of the "most numerous branch of the state legislature." States' own legislatures make laws for their own states. The "most numerous branch of the state legislature" would be that branch or house that had the most members.

When the Constitution was written, the different states had different qualifications as to who could vote. A common qualification was to own property, which is no longer the case. Because each state had its own qualifications, the writers of the Constitution left it up to the states to decide who could vote.

The term used in the Constitution for a person who votes is "elector," which means a person who elects someone, or a qualified voter.

The Fifteenth, Nineteenth, Twenty-fourth and Twenty-sixth Amendments prevented states from denying citizens voting privileges because of gender, race, failure to pay a tax, or age, if they are eighteen years or older.

Section 2. The House of Representatives shall be composed of members chosen every second year by the people of the several [several, in this case, means individual, separate or distinct. The several states refers to the separate, individual states, such as New York, Virginia, Georgia.] **states, and the**

electors [someone who "elects," a qualified voter] **in each state shall have the qualifications requisite** [required or necessary] **for electors** [someone who has the right to vote in an election] **of the most numerous branch of the state legislature.**

No person shall be a representative who shall not have attained [reached] **to the age of twenty five years, and been seven years a citizen of the United States, and who shall not, when elected, be an inhabitant of that state in which he shall be chosen.** [A representative must be 25 years old, a citizen for seven years and a resident of their state.]

Two parts of the following paragraph no longer apply:

1. Taxes are no longer based upon a state's census, but people are now taxed according to their income. This was changed in 1913 with the adoption of the Sixteenth Amendment on income tax.

2. Counting slaves as "three-fifths of all other persons" no longer applies — see pages 50–51 for more details.

The next paragraph still provides that 1) the number of representatives to which each state is entitled shall be based on the population of that state; 2) every ten years the people in the United States must be counted and; 3) each state is entitled to at least one representative.

The first House of Representatives had 65 members, or one representative for every 30,000 people. As the population of the United States increased this proportion needed to be adjusted. In 1929, Congress passed a law limiting the number of members of the House of Representatives to 435. Thus, today we have one representative for approximately every 690,000 people.

Representatives and direct taxes [A "direct tax" is a tax placed on a person or organization. Examples of direct taxes would be income taxes and property taxes where persons or organizations are taxed. An "indirect tax," on the other hand, taxes goods or services. Sales taxes are an example of an indirect tax.] **shall be apportioned** [divided and allocated] **among the several states which may be included within this Union, according to their respective numbers, which shall be determined by adding to the whole number of free persons** [someone who is not a slave]**, including those bound to service for a term of years** ["a person bound to service for a term of years" would be a person who had a contract binding him to work for another person for a given length of time. It was common practice in the 1700s for a person in Britain to sign such a contract and then come to America and work for a number of years in exchange for being brought over to America]**, and excluding Indians not taxed, three-fifths of all other persons. The actual enumeration**

[establishing the number of something. In this case, it would specify how many people live in each state and that number of people would determine how many representatives each state would receive.] **shall be made within three years after the first meeting of the Congress of the United States, and within every subsequent term of ten years, in such a manner as they shall by law direct. The number of representatives shall not exceed one for every thirty thousand, but each state shall have at least one representative; and until such enumeration shall be made, the State of New Hampshire shall be entitled to choose three, Massachusetts eight, Rhode Island and Providence Plantations** [the name of four early settlements in what is now Rhode Island] **one, Connecticut five, New York six, New Jersey four, Pennsylvania eight, Delaware one, Maryland six, Virginia ten, North Carolina five, South Carolina five, and Georgia three.**

The above paragraph states 1) that the number of each state's representatives to the House of Representatives will be allocated based on the number of people living in that state; 2) direct taxes will be allocated to each state based on the number of people living in that state; and 3) that a census will be conducted every ten years to determine these numbers. These numbers are determined by counting slaves as three-fifths of a person. There were roughly 4 million people in the United States when the first census was conducted in 1790; New York State had approximately 340,000 people while Virginia had approximately 690,000. So, New York State got about half as many representatives as Virginia and had to pay about half as much direct tax.

After the Constitution was ratified, Congress first mainly collected revenue by taxing imports of foreign goods shipped into the U.S., and next it taxed goods produced or consumed in the U.S., mainly liquor and tobacco. These were indirect taxes. Much later, direct taxes were collected, such as an income tax during the Civil War from 1862 to 1872 to help finance the war. In 1880, the Supreme Court ruled that this income tax during the Civil War was actually an indirect tax.

An income tax was again passed by Congress in 1894. However, the next year it was held unconstitutional by the Supreme Court because it was considered a direct tax and must be apportioned among the states based on population. Finally, in 1913, the Sixteenth Amendment was passed which gave Congress the power to collect direct taxes without being apportioned by population, and the income tax has been with us ever since. So, there has been some debate, if not confusion, over the years regarding how to collect direct taxes.

When vacancies happen in the representation from any

state, the executive authority thereof [of that state] **shall issue writs** [formal legal documents ordering some action; in this case, ordering an election] **of election to fill such vacancies.**

The House of Representatives shall choose their speaker [the officer presiding over a lawmaking body, such as the House of Representatives] **and other officers; and shall have the sole power of impeachment.** [charging the holder of a public office with misconduct. The House of Representatives makes a written charge against an official. After impeachment the Senate sits as a court, hears evidence and gives a verdict.]

Section 3. The Senate of the United States shall be composed of two senators from each state, chosen by the legislature thereof, for six years; and each senator shall have one vote.

The Seventeenth Amendment to the Constitution changed this paragraph so that the voters in each state elect their own senators, rather than the state legislatures choosing that state's senators.

Senators are elected to six-year terms, unlike representatives who have terms of only two years. All members of the House of Representatives are elected every two years. In the Senate only one-third of the senators are elected every two years. This system prevents the Senate being composed of new and inexperienced members every six years. Now the Senate has one hundred senators since the number of states has increased to fifty. Staggering the elections of these senators allows approximately one-third of them or roughly thirty-three senators to be elected or re-elected every two years.

The section of the next paragraph about filling vacancies in the Senate was modified by the Seventeenth Amendment. Originally, if a vacancy occurred in the Senate, the governor of the state that had a Senate vacancy appointed a temporary senator until that state's legislature chose a permanent one. Now, a state that has a vacancy in the U.S. Senate may empower that state's governor to appoint a temporary senator until the people choose one in a new election.

Immediately after they shall be assembled in consequence [by means of] **of the first election, they shall be divided as equally as may be into three classes. The seats** [places in an elected legislature or other body] **of the senators of the first class shall be vacated at the expiration of the second year, of the second class at the expiration of the fourth year, and of the third class at the expiration of the sixth year, so that one-third may be chosen every second year; and if vacancies happen by resignation, or otherwise, during the recess of the legislature of any state, the executive** [governor] **thereof may make temporary**

appointments until the next meeting of the legislature, which shall then fill such vacancies.

No person shall be a senator who shall not have attained to the age of thirty years, and been nine years a citizen of the United States, and who shall not, when elected, be an inhabitant of that state for which he shall be chosen.

The vice president of the United States shall be president [somebody who is in charge at a meeting] of the Senate, but shall have no vote, unless they be equally divided.

The vice president presides over the Senate. "Preside" means to serve as the chairman of an assembly or exercise control or authority over an assembly. The Speaker of the House of Representatives and the president of the Senate "preside" over those assemblies. The vice president only has the power to vote on Senate matters when the vote is "equally divided," or tied. The vice president has been called upon to vote many times to break ties in the Senate, often on important matters. For example, in 1793 the vice president voted in favor of remaining neutral concerning a war between France and Britain and other European countries.

The Senate shall choose their other officers, and also a president pro tempore ["pro tempore" is a Latin phrase meaning "temporary"], **in the absence of the vice president, or when he shall exercise the office of president of the United States.**

The vice president of the United States serves as the president of the Senate. If the vice president is not present during the meeting of the Senate, the president pro tempore takes his place to run the Senate meeting. In modern times, the vice president generally presides over the Senate only on ceremonial occasions or when a tie-breaking vote is needed.

The Senate shall have the sole power to try [to examine according to law, as in a court] **all impeachments. When sitting** [engaged in its business] **for that purpose, they shall be on oath or affirmation.** [An oath is a formal declaration with an appeal to God for the truth of what is being declared. An affirmation is also a formal legal declaration by a person who declines to take an oath for reasons of conscience.] **When the president of the United States is tried, the chief justice** [the chief judge on the Supreme Court] **shall preside: and no person shall be convicted without the concurrence** [agreement] **of two-thirds of the members present.**

Judgment in cases of impeachment shall not extend further than to removal from office, and disqualification to hold and enjoy any office of honor, trust, or profit

under the United States: but the party convicted shall nevertheless be liable and subject to indictment, trial, judgment and punishment, according to law.

In 1868, President Andrew Johnson was impeached in the House of Representatives, but his trial in the Senate did not result in his conviction and removal from the office of the president because two-thirds of the senators did not vote to convict him. In 1974, President Richard Nixon resigned before he could be impeached in the House and tried in the Senate. In 1998 President Bill Clinton was impeached in the House, but found not guilty in the Senate in 1999.

Section 4. The times, places and manner of holding elections for senators and representatives shall be prescribed [directed] **in each state by the legislature thereof; but the Congress may at any time by law make or alter such regulations, except as to the places of choosing senators.**

Because each individual state's legislature chose that state's senators to the U.S. Senate, the U.S. Congress was not allowed to choose where such elections were to be held, since that would basically be the U.S. Congress telling each state where it had to have its capital and state legislature.

The Congress shall assemble at least once in every year,

and such meeting shall be on the first Monday in December, unless they shall by law appoint a different day.

The writers of the Constitution stipulated that Congress must meet at least once a year because the kings in Europe had been known to keep their parliaments from meeting for years at a time. The Twentieth Amendment changed the opening day for Congress to January 3.

Section 5. Each house shall be the judge of the elections, returns [reports on the count of votes at polling places] **and qualifications of its own members, and a majority** [more than half] **of each shall constitute a quorum** [the minimum number of members of an assembly required to be present to make the actions of that assembly valid.] **to do business; but a smaller number** [less than a quorum] **may adjourn** [postpone action of a convened legislative body until another time specified] **from day to day, and may be authorized to compel the attendance of absent members, in such manner, and under such penalties as each house may provide.**

Each house may determine the rules of its proceedings, punish its members for disorderly behavior, and, with the concurrence of two-thirds, expel a member. These provisions are similar to the practices of the British Parliament.

Each house shall keep a journal of its proceedings, and from time to time publish the same, excepting such parts as may in their judgment require secrecy; and the yeas and nays ["yea" is "yes," or a vote in favor of a proposition; while a "nay" is a "no," or a vote not in favor of a proposition.] **of the members of either house on any question shall, at the desire of one-fifth of those present, be entered on the journal.**

The *Congressional Record*, a daily publication of Congress, contains a complete word-for-word report of what is said in normal sessions of Congress.

Neither house, during the session of Congress, shall, without the consent of the other, adjourn for more than three days, nor to any other place than that in which the two houses shall be sitting.

The two houses of the British Parliament had previously quarreled with each other. If one house adjourned, it would bring Congress to a standstill.

Section 6. The senators and representatives shall receive a compensation for their services, to be ascertained [established] **by law, and paid out of the Treasury of the United States. They shall in all cases, except treason, felony** [a major crime such as murder, arson, rape, etc.] **and breach** [violation] **of the peace** [that quiet, order and security which is guaranteed by the laws], **be privileged** [exempted] **from arrest during their attendance at the session of their respective houses, and in going to and returning from the same; and for any speech or debate in either house, they shall not be questioned in any other place.**

Prior to our Constitution, members of the British Parliament were not paid for their services. This practice prevented poor citizens from becoming members of the British Parliament. U.S. senators and representatives as of 2010 receive annual salaries of $174,000 while some other officers of the Senate and House of Representatives have higher salaries. The Speaker of the House receives a yearly salary of $223,500 and the president of the Senate (who is also the vice president of the U.S.) receives $230,700.

British history also had examples of members of Parliament being punished for speaking what was on their minds.

No senator or representative shall, during the time for which he was elected [during the term of his service in Congress], **be appointed to any civil** [governmental] **office** [a particular duty or employment] **under the authority of the United States, which shall have been created, or the emoluments** [gains from employment or position; payments received for work; salaries, wages, fees, etc.] **whereof** [of which] **shall have been increased during such time; and no person holding any office under the United States, shall be a member of either house during his continuance in office.**

Without this provision, a member of Congress could help create a high-paying job in the federal government and get appointed to that job while still a member of Congress! This provision, disallowing a member of Congress to take another government job when holding a position in Congress, attempts to keep Congress free from outside influence.

Section 7. All bills [proposed laws] **for raising revenue shall originate in the House of Representatives; but the Senate may propose or concur with amendments as on other bills.**

Tax laws are to originate in the House of Representatives, a practice similar to the British Parliament where all tax laws start in the House of Commons, the lower house. The elected members of the House of Commons are more likely to act on behalf of the people who elected them than are the members of the House of Lords, or upper house, which until very recently consisted mainly of nobility who were not elected.

Every bill which shall have passed the House of Representatives and the Senate, shall, before it become

a law, be presented to the president of the United States; if he approve he shall sign it, but if not he shall return it, with his objections to that house in which it shall have originated, who shall enter the objections at large ["at large" in this sense means in complete detail or fully] on their journal, and proceed to reconsider it. If after such reconsideration two-thirds of that house shall agree to pass the bill, it shall be sent, together with the objections, to the other house, by which it shall likewise be reconsidered, and if approved by two-thirds of that house, it shall become a law. But in all such cases the votes of both houses shall be determined by yeas and nays, and the names of the persons voting for and against the bill shall be entered on the journal of each house respectively. If any bill shall not be returned by the president within ten days (Sundays excepted) after it shall have been presented to him, the same shall be a law, in like manner as if he had signed it, unless the Congress by their adjournment prevent its return, in which case it shall not be a law.

This provision lays out how a bill becomes a law. In most of the Colonies before the Revolutionary War, the colonial governors were appointed by the British kings and had the power to reject legislation proposed by the colonial legislatures whose representatives were elected by the colonists. The governors' misuse of this power to reject bills was one of the grievances which led to the revolution.

Every order [command]**, resolution** [formal statement of opinion or intention by a legislature]**, or vote to which the concurrence** [agreement] **of the Senate and House of Representatives may be necessary (except on a question of adjournment) shall be presented to the president of the United States; and before the same shall take effect, shall be approved by him, or being disapproved by him, shall be repassed by two-thirds of the Senate and House of Representatives, according to the rules and limitations prescribed in the case of a bill.**

The above paragraph states that items proposed by Congress should be sent to the president even if they are not named "bills." However, there are several clauses in the Constitution itself that do not require the president's approval, such as the process for amending the Constitution. As a result there has been much legal debate on the interpretation of this paragraph.

The following passages of the Constitution describe the powers of Congress.

Section 8. The Congress shall have power to lay [to set or impose] **and collect taxes, duties** [payments due to the government, especially taxes imposed on imports, exports, or manufactured goods]**, imposts** [taxes, especially taxes on imported goods] **and excises** [taxes on the manufacture, sale, or consumption of various commodities within a country, such as liquor and tobacco], **to pay the debts and provide for the common defense and general welfare of the United States; but all duties, imposts and excises shall be uniform throughout the United States;**

Congress is here granted the power to collect taxes. The section regarding the power to provide for the "general welfare" was used by the Supreme Court to uphold the Social Security Act of 1935, which taxes employers and employees to provide funds for old age, unemployment or disability benefits.

To borrow money on the credit [confidence which people place in the ability of a nation, company or individual to repay borrowed money] **of the United States;**

In 1790, the national debt was $70,000,000 ($70 million). The national debt, or the total amount of money the United States government has borrowed and spent, must be paid back with interest. The national debt includes money the government has borrowed from itself, from U.S. citizens and from foreign citizens and governments.

In 1840, the national debt was $4,000,000 ($4 million).

In 1865 (the last year of the Civil War), the national debt had grown to almost $2,700,000,000 ($2.7 billion).

In 1919 (after World War I), the national debt was $25,500,000,000 ($25.5 billion).

In 1946 (after World War II), the national debt totaled almost $269,500,000,000 ($269.5 billion).

In March 2007, the national debt had increased to more than $8,800,000,000,000 ($8.8 trillion) and $13 trillion by 2010.

To regulate commerce with foreign nations, and among the several states, and with the Indian tribes;

Prior to the Constitution, individual states had been taxing the commerce or trade between themselves. This clause prevents individual states from interfering with trade between states.

To establish a uniform rule of naturalization, and uniform laws on the subject of bankruptcies throughout the United States;

To coin money, regulate the value thereof, and of foreign coin, and fix the standard of weights [such as ounces, pounds, etc.] **and measures** [such as inches, feet, yards, acres, etc.]**;**

"To coin money" means, literally, to make coins. The authors of the Constitution had lost confidence in paper money during the Revolutionary War, but expected that banks would issue paper money that could be redeemed in gold or silver.

In 1913, the U.S. Congress passed a law that delegated the right to create money to the Federal Reserve System. This unusual mixture of public and private ownership is directed by a Board of Governors, located in Washington, D.C. At the next level are twelve Federal Reserve Banks, which are legally private corporations, whose stockholders are commercial banks that are members of the Federal Reserve System. The president of the U.S. appoints the seven members of the Board of Governors of the Federal Reserve System, and the Senate must confirm them. They serve fourteen-year terms. The Board of Governors supervises the operations of the twelve regional Federal Reserve Banks and has a major influence on the United States' financial system.

To provide for the punishment of counterfeiting the securities [IOUs, such as savings bonds issued by the U.S. government] **and current coin of the United States;**

To establish post offices and post roads [roads over which mail is carried];

To promote the progress of science and useful arts, by securing for limited times to authors and inventors the exclusive right to their respective writings and discoveries;

Copyrights (the rights of authors and artists to control the use of their works) and patents (exclusive rights to market or use inventions) are covered in the above clause.

To constitute tribunals [courts] **inferior to the Supreme Court;**

Each state has a court system to deal with matters concerning state law. The federal government's court system deals with federal laws. The lowest level, the Federal District Court, is divided so as to serve different geographic areas or "districts" of the United States.

A dispute among different people or organizations, which is to be decided in a court of law, is called a court case or a case. The parties to a case heard at a Federal District Court may appeal that decision to the next higher level of federal courts, the Courts of Appeals. "Appeal" means to make a request to a higher court, asking that a case be reheard or reviewed. There is a Court of Appeals in each of the eleven districts into which the United States is divided, plus a Court of Appeals for the District of Columbia.

The parties to a case heard at a Court of Appeals may appeal that decision to the Supreme Court of the United States in Washington, D.C. The Supreme Court does not review all cases sent to it, but each year selects a few cases from the thousands it receives.

There are other specialized federal courts, but the majority of federal court cases are heard in the above-described courts.

To define and punish piracies and felonies committed on the high seas [the open ocean not under the jurisdiction of a country], **and offenses against the law of nations** [rules that regulate dealings between nations coming from principles of justice, customs or agreements between nations];

The federal government, not the states, has the power to deal with crimes committed on the high seas. Pirates from the North African ports of Morocco, Algiers, Tripoli and Tunis on the Mediterranean Sea interfered with American shipping in the late 1700s. European countries paid money to these pirates so they would not attack their shipping. The United States did the same. When these pirates broke their treaty, the United States sent warships to Tripoli in 1801 and to Algiers in 1815. These actions were instrumental in stopping this piracy.

To declare war, grant letters of marque [a written permission to go outside the jurisdiction of a country to seize the property of people of another country] **and reprisal** [the taking of property and people from an enemy. Letters of marque and reprisal are no longer used. However, these were government documents authorizing an individual to arm a ship and capture enemy merchant ships and cargo.], **and make rules concerning captures on land and water;**

The Constitution gives Congress the power to declare war, but, without a declaration of war by Congress, some presidents have involved the United States in wars: the Korean War (1950-1953), the Vietnam War (1957-1975) and, in more recent years, the Iraq and Afghanistan wars.

To raise and support armies, but no appropriation [money set aside for a particular use] **of money to that use shall be for a longer term than two years;**

Article II of the Constitution makes the president the commander in chief of the army and navy. However, the above paragraph gives Congress the power to appropriate money for military use, but only for two years at a time. In this way, the president cannot continue a war without Congressional funding.

To provide [make available for use] **and maintain a navy;**

To make rules for the government [direction] **and regulation of the land and naval forces;**

To provide [make adequate preparation; enable or allow] **for calling forth the militia** [body of soldiers organized from the civilian population in times of emergencies. When they are not needed for military duties, they pursue their usual occupations.] **to execute the laws of the Union** [the United States of America], **suppress insurrections** [violent uprisings against authority or government] **and repel invasions;**

To provide for organizing, arming, and disciplining, the militia, and for governing such part of them as may be employed in the service of the United States, reserving [retaining] **to the states respectively** [separately or individually], **the appointment of the officers, and the authority of training the militia according to the discipline** [education and instruction] **prescribed by Congress;**

To exercise exclusive legislation in all cases whatsoever, over such district (not exceeding ten miles square) as may, **by cession** [the action of transferring the title or ownership of something to another owner] **of particular states, and the acceptance of Congress, become the seat** [here, "seat" means a location or site] **of the government of the United States,**

and to exercise like authority over all places purchased by the consent of the legislature of the state in which the same shall be, for the erection of forts, magazines [places of storage or military supply depots]**, arsenals** [places for making or storing weapons and other munitions]**, dockyards, and other needful buildings;—and**

The U.S. Congress acts as the legislature for areas owned by the federal government such as U.S. Army bases, Navy bases and Washington, D.C. The District of Columbia ("D.C."), a federal district, does not belong to any state. The city of Washington, located within this federal district, is generally called Washington, D.C. The states of Maryland and Virginia gave this land to the United States government.

To make all laws which shall be necessary and proper for carrying into execution [the putting into operation] **the foregoing powers** [rights or authorities]**, and all other powers vested by this Constitution in the government of the United States, or in any department or officer thereof.**

This clause allows Congress to pass laws to deal with conditions unforeseen at the time it was written, more than 200 years ago.

Section 9. The migration or importation of such persons as any of the states now existing shall think proper to admit, shall not be prohibited by the Congress prior to the year one thousand eight hundred and eight, but a tax or duty may be imposed on such importation, not exceeding ten dollars for each person.

Slave dealers and owners did not want Congress to ban the importation of slaves until the year 1808. This paragraph was placed in the Constitution as a compromise between the northern states, which wanted to stop the slave trade, and the southern states, which wanted the slave trade to continue. In 1808 Congress did stop the slave trade into the United States.

The privilege of the writ [a written legal order] **of habeas corpus** [Latin for "you are ordered to have the body." A writ of habeas corpus is a legal document ordering a person to be brought before a court; specifically, an order requiring that a detained person be brought before a court at a stated time and place to decide the legality of his detention or imprisonment.] **shall not be suspended, unless when in cases of rebellion or invasion the public safety may require it.**

The right of habeas corpus safeguards a person against illegal detention or imprisonment—as such it guarantees personal freedom. It prevents a person from being thrown in jail and forgotten. Some legal authorities consider it the fundamental right, because if a person is left to rot in jail, they have no freedom, let alone freedom of speech or other basic rights.

Earlier in Britain, people were thrown into jail and left there without formal charges brought against them. The writers of the Constitution made sure that this could not legally happen in the United States.

No bill of attainder [a law passed against a person that takes away civil rights and property without a trial] **or ex post facto** [after the fact] **law** [an *ex post facto law* is one which applies to actions committed before the law was passed. Taken from a Latin phrase meaning "from a thing done afterward."] **shall be passed.**

Starting in the 1400s, the English Parliament passed bills that allowed a person to be tried, convicted and sentenced, without a court and judge hearing witnesses testify against him and without proper rules of evidence. The person so charged lost his property and, if he was executed, he could not pass his property to his children. British kings used bills of attainder to get rid of people they disapproved of, although these people had broken no existing laws. Bills of attainder were also passed in the thirteen Colonies during the time of the Revolutionary War. The writers of the Constitution knew how unjust bills of attainder and ex post facto laws were and included this directive against them.

No capitation [a tax, fee, or charge of the same amount for every person] **or other direct tax shall be laid** [to lay, in this sense, means to impose a burden or penalty]**, unless in proportion to the census or enumeration** [the act of counting] **herein before directed to be taken.**

The states that had slaves insisted that this provision be put into the Constitution, as they feared Congress would attempt to collect heavy taxes on slave owners. The above paragraph basically repeats Article I, Section 2 where the Constitution says direct taxes must be apportioned according to the population of the states.

No tax or duty shall be laid on articles exported from any state.

This clause was included in the Constitution because the Southern states feared that Congress would place an export tax on their agricultural products.

No preference shall be given by any regulation of commerce or revenue to the ports of one state over those of another; nor shall vessels bound to, or from, one state,

be obliged to enter, clear, or pay duties in another.

Because Maryland feared that the new government would pass laws favoring the ports of Virginia, it influenced this prohibition against Congress making laws concerning trade favoring one state over another.

No money shall be drawn from the Treasury, but in consequence [as a result] **of appropriations made by law; and a regular statement and account of the receipts and expenditures of all public money shall be published from time to time.**

Money cannot be taken from the Treasury without having been approved by Congress and agreed to by the president. British history had many examples of financial disaster when a king or Parliament spent money indiscriminately.

No title of nobility shall be granted by the United States; and no person holding any office of profit or trust under them ["them" refers to the United States; "no person holding any office of profit or trust under them" means any federal official] **shall, without the consent of the Congress, accept any present, emolument, office, or title, of any kind whatever, from any king, prince or foreign state.**

At the end of the Revolutionary War in 1783, some

soldiers wanted George Washington to accept the title of king. He refused. Neither may any government employee accept presents or other similar benefits from another country without Congressional approval.

Section 10. No state shall enter into any treaty, alliance, or confederation [a group of nations or states joined in a league, as for common defense]**; grant letters of marque and reprisal; coin money; emit** [issue formally and with authority; put into circulation] **bills of credit** [a "bill of credit" is paper money]**; make any thing but gold and silver coin a tender in payment of debts; pass any bill of attainder, ex post facto law, or law impairing the obligation of contracts** [laws cannot be passed that alter or make illegal existing contracts]**, or grant any title of nobility.**

One of the problems with the Articles of Confederation was that states issued their own paper money, which became almost worthless. The Constitution forbids states from issuing paper money.

The next clause basically says that states may not interfere with trade between the states. States require Congressional approval to collect taxes on trade going into or out of a state, except for inspection fees.

No state shall, without the consent of the Congress, lay

any imposts or duties on imports or exports, except what may be absolutely necessary for executing its inspection laws; and the net [remaining from an amount of money after all deductions have been made] produce [that which is yielded] of all duties and imposts, laid by any state on imports or exports, shall be for the use of the Treasury of the United States; and all such laws shall be subject to the revision and control of the Congress.

The next clause contains rights which an independent government would have. The Constitution gives these rights to the federal government, not the states, making the states part of one nation and not independent nations.

No state shall, without the consent of Congress, lay any duty of tonnage [a tax on ships at so much per ton of cargo], keep troops, or ships of war in time of peace, enter into any agreement or compact [contract or treaty] with another state, or with a foreign power, or engage in war, unless actually invaded, or in such imminent danger as will not admit [allow] of delay.

Article II.

Section 1. The executive power shall be vested in a president of the United States of America. He shall hold his office during the term of four years and, together with

the vice president, chosen for the same term, be elected, as follows:

The next several clauses establish the system by which presidents and vice presidents are elected in the United States. The persons writing the Constitution debated at length how these leaders should be chosen. Should they be selected by the U.S. Congress; by the governors of the states; by the state legislatures (in which cases the president would be under the control of the U.S. Congress, the state governors or the state legislatures); or by the votes of the people?

The Constitution outlined a system for electing presidents called the Electoral College. Here, "college" means an organized group with particular aims, duties and privileges. "Electoral" means relating to elections or electors. The term "Electoral College" designates the group of people that elects the president and vice president.

The word "elector," although used in two slightly different ways in the Constitution, carries the same basic meaning: "someone who elects." When a U.S. citizen votes in an election, he is an "elector" or a qualified voter. A slightly different usage applies this word to the person who votes at the Electoral College.

Under the Electoral College system, each state is allocated a number of electors equal to the number of Congressional representatives and senators of that state. Those electors elect the president and vice president. For example, if a state has twenty representatives to the U.S. House of Representatives and two U.S. senators, that state would be allowed twenty-two electors.

The Constitution does not state how the electors are to be chosen, but left that up to the states. However, the Constitution does say the electors must not be government officials—the purpose of this is so government officials cannot themselves select the electors who will elect the president and vice president.

The electors from each state were chosen in a variety of ways, such as by the individual state legislatures. Regardless of how the electors were chosen, however, the American populace did not directly elect the president.

This system was originally developed out of the belief that the average man was incapable of wisely selecting a leader. Thus, the writers of the Constitution decided that a group of enlightened (and generally wealthy) community leaders would select the president on the people's behalf. George Washington, first president, was chosen by this method.

Each state shall appoint, in such manner as the legislature thereof may direct, a number of electors [people who are chosen to vote at the Electoral College], **equal to the whole number of senators and representatives to which the state may be entitled in the Congress; but no senator or representative, or person holding an office of trust or profit under the United States, shall be appointed an elector.**

The Electoral College never meets as a single group. Instead, the electors from each state meet in their own capital and cast their votes which are then sent to the U.S. Congress for a final count.

Each elector cast two different votes for president. The person receiving the most votes became the president, while the one receiving the second highest became vice president. If no candidate for president received a majority of votes or there was a tie, the House of Representatives chose the president and vice president; if there was a tie for vice president in the House, the Senate chose the vice president. The Twelfth Amendment changes this so that the electors cast one vote for president and one for vice president.

The electors shall meet in their respective states, and vote by ballot for two persons, of whom one at least shall not be an inhabitant of the same state with themselves. And

they shall make a list of all the persons voted for, and of the number of votes for each; which list they shall sign and certify [make a declaration in writing], and transmit sealed to the seat of the government of the United States, directed to the president of the Senate. The president of the Senate shall, in the presence of the Senate and House of Representatives, open all the certificates [declarations made in writing and signed by the person and intended to verify a fact] and the votes shall then be counted. The person having the greatest number of votes shall be the president, if such number be a majority of the whole number of electors appointed; and if there be more than one who have such majority, and have an equal number of votes [in this system, each elector voted for two people, so it was possible for more than one person to get a majority and these people have the same number of votes.], then the House of Representatives shall immediately choose by ballot one of them for president; and if no person have a majority, then from the five highest on the list, the said house shall, in like manner, choose the president. But in choosing the president, the votes shall be taken by states, the representation from each state having one vote; a quorum for this purpose shall consist of a member or members from two-thirds of the states, and a majority of all the states shall be necessary to a choice. In every case, after the choice of the president, the person having the greatest number of votes of the electors shall be the vice president. But if there should remain two or more who have equal votes, the Senate shall choose from them by ballot the vice president.

The Congress may determine the time of choosing the electors, and the day on which they shall give their votes; which day shall be the same throughout the United States.

No person except a natural born citizen, or a citizen of the United States, at the time of the adoption of this Constitution, shall be eligible to the office of president; neither shall any person be eligible to that office, who shall not have attained to the age of 35 years, and been 14 years a resident within the United States.

In case of the removal of the president from office, or of his death, resignation, or inability to discharge the powers and duties of the said office, the same shall devolve [pass to a body or person at a lower level (said of duties and responsibilities)] on the vice president, and the Congress may by law provide for the case of removal, death, resignation, or inability, both of the president and vice president, declaring what officer shall then act as president, and such officer shall act accordingly, until the disability be removed, or a president shall be elected.

The previous paragraph was later modified by the Twenty-fifth Amendment, which gave a different procedure to be followed in case a president or vice president were removed or unable to hold the office.

The president shall, at stated times, receive for his services, a compensation, which shall neither be increased nor diminished during the period for which he shall have been elected, and he shall not receive within that period any other emolument from the United States, or any of them.

In 1789, the first Congress set the salary of the president at $25,000 per year. Today, the president receives a taxable salary of $400,000. In addition, he receives an expense allowance of $50,000; travel allowance and other allowances to fulfill his duties. The president cannot receive other monies for personal use from the federal government or from any state while he is president so that he cannot be corrupted by sums of money from other areas of the government.

Before he enter on the execution of his office, he shall take the following oath or affirmation:

"I do solemnly swear (or affirm) that I will faithfully execute the office of president of the United States, and will

to the best of my ability, preserve, protect and defend the Constitution of the United States."

Section 2. The president shall be commander in chief [supreme commander] of the army and navy of the United States, and of the militia of the several states, when called into the actual service of the United States; he may require the opinion, in writing, of the principal officer in each of the executive departments, upon any subject relating to the duties of their respective offices, and he shall have power to grant reprieves ["to grant reprieves" means to allow postponements of punishments] and pardons [lessening or setting aside the punishment for a crime] for offenses against the United States, except in cases of impeachment.

He shall have power, by and with the advice and consent of the Senate, to make treaties, provided two-thirds of the senators present concur [agree]; and he shall nominate, and by and with the advice and consent of the Senate, shall appoint ambassadors [a government official of the highest rank sent by one nation to live in another nation as its representative], other public ministers [government officials representing their own government in another country and ranking below an ambassador] and consuls [government officials appointed to aide their own country's business interests, and citizens in a foreign country], judges of the

Supreme Court, and all other officers [people appointed to positions of rank or authority in the government or military] **of the United States, whose appointments are not herein otherwise provided for, and which shall be established by law; but the Congress may by law vest the appointment of such inferior officers** [government officials of lower rank than ambassadors, Supreme Court judges, etc.], **as they think proper, in the president alone, in the courts of law, or in the heads of departments.**

The president has the power to make treaties, if approved by the Senate, and to nominate major officers such as ambassadors and Supreme Court judges.

The president shall have power to fill up all vacancies that may happen during the recess [suspension of business] **of the Senate, by granting commissions** [authorizations to perform certain duties and take on certain powers], **which shall expire at the end of their next session.**

The president can make temporary appointments or commissions to offices, which require Senate confirmation when the Senate is in recess or not in session.

Section 3. He shall from time to time give to the Congress information of the state of the Union, and recommend to

their consideration such measures [actions to be taken] **as he shall judge necessary and expedient** [proper under the circumstances]**; he may, on extraordinary occasions, convene** [to cause to assemble] **both houses, or either** [one or the other] **of them, and in case of disagreement between them, with respect to the time of adjournment, he may adjourn them to such time as he shall think proper; he shall receive ambassadors and other public ministers; he shall take care that the laws be faithfully executed, and shall commission all the officers of the United States.**

The phrase "he shall take care that the laws be faithfully executed" means that it is the president's responsibility to ensure that the laws of the United States—with the Constitution being the supreme law from which all other laws derive—are carefully followed.

Federal officials (meaning people who are *appointed* to their position rather than *elected*), both civilian and military, get their authority from the authority of the president.

Section 4. The president, vice president, and all civil officers of the United States shall be removed from office on impeachment for, and conviction of, treason, bribery, or other high crimes [great offenses] **and misdemeanors** [offenses less serious than crimes].

Article III.

Section 1. The judicial power of the United States shall be vested in one Supreme Court, and in such inferior courts as the Congress may, from time to time, ordain and establish. The judges, both of the supreme and inferior courts, shall hold their offices during good behavior, and shall, at stated times, receive for their services a compensation, which shall not be diminished during their continuance in office.

Supreme Court and other federal judges are appointed by the president and hold office for as long as they wish. The president cannot dismiss them. They can, however, be impeached by the House of Representatives and tried by the Senate for offenses, and if found guilty by the Senate, dismissed from office. Their salaries cannot be cut while they are in office. These rules help keep the judges free from the pressure of making decisions demanded by Congress or the president. The chief justice as of 2010 receives a yearly salary of $217,000, while the other eight justices receive a salary of $208,000 per year.

Section 2. The judicial power shall extend to all cases [matters to be decided], **in law** [rules established by governments for regulating people's actions] **and equity** ["equity" means fairness or justice. Equity is a system of rules that supplements and replaces laws in the United States when such laws are inadequate for fair settlement. Based on principles of reason and fairness, equity allows the law to be adjusted to special circumstances. Originally, courts of equity were different from courts of law. Today, most states have combined the equity and law courts into one court system.] **arising under this Constitution, the laws of the United States, and treaties made, or which shall be made under their authority; to all cases affecting ambassadors, other public ministers and consuls; to all cases of admiralty and maritime jurisdiction** [maritime—related to the sea or sailing—and admiralty jurisdiction covers things done upon and relating to the sea, lakes and rivers. These include transactions relating to commerce and navigation, as well as damages and injuries. Formerly this law was administered by admirals, which explains its name.]**; to controversies** [lawsuits] **to which the United States shall be a party; to controversies between two or more states; between a state and citizens of another state; between citizens of different states; between citizens of the same state, claiming lands under grants of different states; and between a state, or the citizens thereof, and foreign states, citizens or subjects.**

From this section, which has been expanded by later Supreme Court decisions, the Supreme Court receives the authority to declare laws "unconstitutional" if they do not agree with the Constitution.

The Eleventh Amendment changed Section 2 above slightly, so that a citizen of one state cannot sue another state in a federal court.

In all cases affecting ambassadors, other public ministers and consuls, and those in which a state shall be party, the Supreme Court shall have original jurisdiction ["original jurisdiction" is the authority to try a case from its beginning. Cases affecting these types of people listed above must begin at the Supreme Court]. **In all the other cases before mentioned, the Supreme Court shall have appellate** [relating to appeals, which are reviews of lower court decisions by a higher court] **jurisdiction, both as to law and fact, with such exceptions, and under such regulations as the Congress shall make.** [Any case other than the types mentioned in the first sentence of this paragraph must be started in a lower court after which the Supreme Court may review or examine the lower court's decision. Congress may pass laws that regulate or create exceptions to this.]

The trial of all crimes, except in cases of impeachment, shall be by jury; and such trial shall be held in the state where the said crimes shall have been committed; but when

not committed within any state, the trial shall be at such place or places as the Congress may by law have directed.

The Declaration of Independence stated that many American colonists had been deprived of trials by jury. Now if the Constitution is followed, this can no longer happen.

Impeachments are to be tried in the Senate. Criminal trials are to be held in the state where the crime took place or, if the crime did not take place in a state, but on the high seas, for example, Congress may decide where the trial should take place.

Section 3. Treason against the United States shall consist only in levying [making] **war against them, or in adhering** [being attached as a follower] **to their enemies, giving them aid and comfort. No person shall be convicted of treason unless on the testimony of two witnesses to the same overt act** ["overt" means open or public. "Overt act" is a legal term which means an actual open and outward action taken to further a crime. For example, thinking about pulling out a gun and robbing someone would not be an overt act; actually pulling out a gun and robbing someone would be an overt act.] **or on confession in open court.**

To be found guilty of treason against the U.S., two witnesses must have seen the accused person commit the treason or, in open court, the accused person must confess to the treason.

Talking or thinking about treason is not a treasonable act; "treason" means actually doing something treasonous.

The Congress shall have power to declare the punishment of treason, but no attainder [the loss of a person's civil rights and property because he has been sentenced to death or outlawed] **of treason shall work corruption of blood** ["but no attainder of treason shall work corruption of blood" means that a blood relative or family member of a person guilty of treason shall not be held guilty of his or her relative's treason. In times prior to this, sometimes a traitor's family members were also punished.] **or forfeiture** [a giving up of something as a penalty, such as losing one's property as a payment for a crime], **except during the life of the person attainted** [punished by attainder].

Congress declares what the punishment for treason shall be. The family of a traitor cannot share the guilt—and a person convicted of treason can lose or forfeit property only during his lifetime. This clause will not allow a traitor's family to be unfairly punished. As an example of the last sentence, the property of a Confederate general had been seized during the U.S. Civil War. The general had a son as an heir. The Supreme Court held that under the above clause, the purchaser of the general's property had to give the property to the general's son when the general died.

Article IV.

Section 1. Full faith [belief; confidence; trust] **and credit** [a reliance on the truth of something said or done] **shall be given in each state to the public** [in open view] **acts, records and judicial proceedings of every other state. And the Congress may by general laws prescribe** ["prescribe" in this sense means order or direct] **the manner in which such acts, records and proceedings shall be proved, and the effect thereof.**

Each individual state's laws, records and court decisions need to be respected by other states. This prevents a person from moving between states to escape his responsibilities.

Section 2. The citizens of each state shall be entitled to all privileges and immunities of citizens in the several states.

A person living in one state can move to another state and have all the rights and privileges of the people in the state he moved to.

A person charged in any state with treason, felony, or other crime, who shall flee from justice, and be found in another state, shall, on demand of the executive authority of the state from which he fled, be delivered up, to be removed to the state having jurisdiction of the crime.

The next clause was no longer necessary after the Thirteenth Amendment abolished slavery. However, this paragraph states that a slave fleeing from one state to another must be returned to the state he fled from. This was put into the Constitution so that the southern states, who wanted to prevent their slaves from escaping to the northern states to gain their freedom, would ratify the Constitution.

No person held to service or labor in one state, under the laws thereof, escaping into another, shall, in consequence [as a result] **of any law or regulation therein** [in that place; referring to the state where the slave escaped to], **be discharged from such service or labor, but shall be delivered up on claim of the party to whom such service or labor may be due.**

Section 3. New states may be admitted by the Congress into this Union, but no new state shall be formed or erected within the jurisdiction of any other state, nor any state be formed by the junction [act of joining] **of two or more states, or parts of states, without the consent of the legislatures of the states concerned, as well as of the Congress.**

All of the land that now makes up the United States did not belong to the country at the time the Constitution was written. This section allowed new states to be admitted to the United States. As a result of the Revolutionary War, the

United States acquired from Great Britain all land from the Atlantic coast to the Mississippi River.

In 1803, a vast amount of land from the Mississippi River to the Rocky Mountains was purchased from France.

In 1819, Florida was purchased from Spain.

In 1845, the former independent Republic of Texas became the 28th state.

The land in the northwestern part of the United States was acquired from Great Britain in 1846.

Between 1846 and 1847 the United States was at war with Mexico. After the United States invaded Mexico and captured Mexico City, Mexico gave up its claim to the land west of the Rocky Mountains in exchange for a payment of $15 million.

In 1867 Alaska was purchased from Russia and became a state in 1960.

In 1898 the Hawaiian Islands were annexed by the United States, becoming a territory in 1900 and a state in 1959.

This section also says that new states cannot be formed by splitting or joining existing states. However, during the Civil War from 1861 to 1865, the state of Virginia fought against the northern states, while the people in the western part of Virginia fought on the side of the northern states against the southern states. Following the Civil War, Congress allowed West Virginia to be its own state, since, in contrast to Virginia, it had not rebelled against the United States.

The Congress shall have power to dispose of ["dispose of" means to deal conclusively with, or settle] **and make all needful rules and regulations respecting the territory or other property belonging to the United States; and nothing in this Constitution shall be so construed as to prejudice** ["to prejudice," here means to injure, or harm because of some action] **any claims of the United States, or of any particular state.** [This last part was included because, at the time the Constitution was drafted, North Carolina and Georgia had claims on lands to the west of them.]

Congress has used the power granted to it from the previous clause to govern territories owned by the United States, but which had not become states, such as Puerto Rico.

Section 4. The United States shall guarantee to every state in this Union a republican form of government [a republican form of government is one in which the people are represented in the government by their representatives], **and shall protect each of them against invasion; and**

on application [formal request to an authority] **of the legislature, or of the executive (when the legislature cannot be convened), against domestic violence.**

A republican form of government allows the people's representatives to make the laws and administer them. The federal government has responsibility for protecting the states from invasion by foreign countries. Federal troops may be sent to a state to deal with "domestic violence" or rioting of people in a state.

Article V.

The Congress, whenever two-thirds of both houses shall deem [conclude] **it necessary, shall propose amendments to this Constitution, or on the application of the legislatures of two-thirds of the several states, shall call a convention for proposing amendments, which, in either case, shall be valid to all intents and purposes, as part of this Constitution, when ratified by the legislatures of three-fourths of the several states, or by conventions** [meetings of delegates or representatives for consultation on important issues] **in three-fourths thereof, as the one or the other mode** [manner; method] **of ratification may be proposed by the Congress; provided that no amendment which may be made prior to the year one thousand eight hundred and eight shall**

in any manner affect the first and fourth clauses in the ninth section of the first article [the first clause deals with importing slaves and the fourth deals with taxes]**; and that no state, without its consent, shall be deprived of its equal suffrage** [the right to vote] **in the Senate.**

Article V tells how the Constitution can be amended or changed. This was the first time in history a government provided for such changes without violence or bloodshed.

Thus far, all amendments to the Constitution were proposed by Congress and not by state legislatures. All ratifications of amendments that have passed have been done by state legislatures except for the Twenty-first Amendment (which repealed prohibition of alcohol and which was ratified by state conventions).

Several movements to convene a constitutional convention developed in the 1970s and 1980s. One movement wanted to forbid abortions to women. Another wanted to make a balanced U.S. federal budget mandatory. By 1987, thirty-two state legislatures had voted in favor of calling such a convention.

This fell two states short of the thirty-four needed to comprise the three-fourths of the states necessary to call such a convention.

Several states voted against or cancelled their call for a constitutional convention out of fear that it could become a "runaway" convention—meaning that the constitutional convention could go beyond dealing with matters concerning a balanced federal budget. It might try to totally re-write the Constitution.

This article also made it impossible to abolish importing slaves prior to 1808 and made it impossible to take away a state's voting rights in the Senate without that state's consent.

Article VI.

All debts contracted and engagements [obligations by agreement or contract] **entered into, before the adoption of this Constitution, shall be as valid against the United States under this Constitution, as under the Confederation.** ["Confederation" refers to the United States before the Constitution was adopted. Then the Articles of Confederation were the basis for our national government.]

The United States was obligated to pay its debts—even those debts incurred before the adoption of the Constitution, when the United States was still governed by the Articles of Confederation, prior to 1788.

This Constitution, and the laws of the United States

which shall be made in pursuance [the carrying out of something in the way that is expected or required] **thereof; and all treaties made, or which shall be made, under the authority of the United States, shall be the supreme law of the land; and the judges in every state shall be bound thereby** ["thereby" means by or through that. In this case, "that" is referring to the Constitution], **any thing in the Constitution or laws of any state to the contrary notwithstanding** [without being affected by the particular factor mentioned].

This makes clear that the Constitution is the supreme law of the land. Further, that all laws of the United States shall be in agreement with and uphold the U.S. Constitution. For example, prior to the Eighteenth Amendment, which prohibited the sale and manufacture of intoxicating alcohol, many state and federal laws governed the sale and manufacture of alcohol and much money was gained through taxes by the states and the federal government from the sale and manufacture of alcohol. However, all these laws were no longer in effect once the Eighteenth Amendment was ratified.

All state judges are also bound to uphold the U.S. Constitution.

The senators and representatives before mentioned, and the members of the several state legislatures, and all executive and judicial officers, both of the United States and of the several states, shall be bound by oath or affirmation, to support this Constitution; but no religious test shall ever be required as a qualification to any office or public trust under the United States.

All federal and state government officers must take an oath that they will support the Constitution. No one can be denied a government position because of his religious beliefs.

Article VII.

The ratification of the conventions of nine states, shall be sufficient for the establishment of this Constitution between the states so ratifying the same.

Done in convention by the unanimous consent of the states present the seventeenth day of September in the year of our Lord one thousand seven hundred and eighty-seven and of the independence of the United States of America the twelfth. ["The twelfth" here means the twelfth year of independence for the United States.] **In witness whereof we have hereunto** [to this document] **subscribed** [signed at the end of a document] **our names.**

The Constitution was written in 1787, twelve years after the United States gained its independence, and was signed by the delegates to the Constitutional Convention on September 17—which is now celebrated as Constitution Day. It was ratified in 1788 when conventions in nine states approved it, and put into effect in 1789. By 1790 all thirteen states had approved it. The first person to sign the Constitution was George Washington, one of the representatives from Virginia, who served as the president of the Constitutional Convention. Two years later he became the first president of the United States.

Amendments to the Constitution

In 1789 the very First Congress of the United States proposed to the state legislatures twelve amendments to the U.S. Constitution. The first of these amendments dealt with the members of the House of Representatives, and never became part of the Constitution. The second, limiting the ability of Congress to increase the salaries of its members, was not ratified until 1992 when it became the Twenty-seventh Amendment.

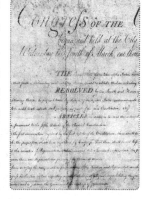

The remaining ten amendments fulfilled the Founder's promise to strengthen the protection of individual rights that was made during the debates over ratification of the Constitution. These ten amendments were ratified and became part of the Constitution in 1791. They are known as the "Bill of Rights" and remain today as the primary protection of the rights of the American people.

The Bill of Rights limits the federal government's powers to unreasonably interfere with people's rights to go about their lives as they see fit. All of the fifty states have written into their constitutions similar bills of rights to limit each state government's powers. The rights of individuals to be protected from interference by other individuals, companies or groups are reflected in other federal, state and local laws, as well.

The Preamble to the Bill of Rights states the purpose of these amendments and the reason they were added to the Constitution.

The original text of the preamble and amendments is printed in **bold type**. Definitions and commentary are in regular type and enclosed in [square brackets] when they appear within the text of the original. The Bill of Rights and its preamble can be seen and read in their original wording without definitions and a minimum of commentary in the Appendix of this book.

Congress of the United States

begun and held at the City of New York [Washington, D.C. did not become the capital of the United States until 1800. In 1789, the U.S. Congress met in New York]**, on Wednesday the fourth of March, one thousand seven hundred and eighty-nine.**

THE Conventions of a number of the States, having at the time of their adopting the Constitution, expressed a desire, in order to prevent misconstruction [interpreting something such as words or actions incorrectly; mistaking the true meaning] or abuse of its powers, that further declaratory and restrictive clauses should be added: And as extending the ground [foundation; that which supports anything] of public confidence in the Government, will best ensure the beneficent [causing good to be done] ends [intended purposes] of its institution [action of setting something in motion or establishing something].

RESOLVED by the Senate and House of Representatives of the United States of America, in Congress assembled, two-thirds of both Houses concurring, that the following Articles be proposed to the Legislatures of the several States, as amendments to the Constitution of the United States, all, or any of which Articles, when ratified by three-fourths of the said Legislatures, to be valid to all intents and purposes, as part of the said Constitution; viz [a contraction of a Latin word meaning "that is to say"].

ARTICLES in addition to, and Amendment of the Constitution of the United States of America, proposed by Congress, and ratified by the Legislatures of the several States, pursuant to the fifth Article of the original Constitution.

Amendment 1.

Congress shall make no law respecting [regarding] **an establishment of religion, or prohibiting the free exercise thereof; or abridging** [reducing or restricting] **the freedom of speech, or of the press; or the right of the people peaceably to assemble, and to petition the government for a redress of grievances.**

The English Parliament passed laws in the 1600s to compel all persons to attend the Church of England. Those who were not members of this church were harshly treated. These laws prompted many persons to come to America to escape religious persecution.

That Congress shall make no law "respecting an establishment of religion" or "prohibiting the free exercise thereof" are two rules that fix in place a balance where the government has no authority to tell Americans what to believe regarding their religions and that Americans have a right to express and practice their religions as they see fit. This is a unique set of rights compared to other countries that have national religions. Public opinion polls have shown that the United States is one of the most religious countries in the world.

However, the Supreme Court interpreted these rights

not to be absolute. For example, in the 1880s the Supreme Court held that the laws prohibiting polygamy (having more than one wife at one time) prevented practicing polygamy as a religious belief.

Freedom of speech or of the press also are not absolute rights, but have reasonable restrictions. For example, it is not permissible to spread outright falsehoods in the media about someone or to shout "fire" in a crowded theatre as a practical joke and cause a panic.

English rulers prevented free expression of people's opinions and beliefs by controlling the press. In a democracy, the right to communicate is essential, as is the right to peaceably assemble. We also have the right to petition the government, usually done by submitting a petition signed by numerous supporters, sending a letter, personally visiting a government official or participating in a public demonstration.

Amendment 2.

A well-regulated militia being necessary to the security of a free state, the right of the people to keep and bear arms, shall not be infringed.

The militia could be called together quickly when needed

during the Revolutionary War because citizens possessed their own weapons. This amendment preserves the right of the people to have weapons for their protection.

Amendment 3.

No soldier shall, in time of peace, be quartered in any house without the consent of the owner, nor in time of war, but in a manner to be prescribed by law.

The British forced colonists to house British soldiers in their homes. This amendment was adopted to prevent the United States government from doing the same thing.

Amendment 4.

The right of the people to be secure [safe] **in their persons, houses, papers, and effects** [personal belongings], **against unreasonable searches and seizures, shall not be violated, and no warrants shall issue, but upon probable cause** ["probable cause" means a valid reason in presuming someone is guilty of some illegal act], **supported by oath or affirmation, and particularly describing the place to be searched, and the persons or things to be seized.**

Earlier, in Great Britain and in the thirteen Colonies, the government could search any person or place it wanted to search without legitimate cause or reason.

This amendment, however, only protects people from "unreasonable" government intrusion. It is not considered unreasonable for the police to look into a person's car or house after an arrest or to follow a suspected criminal across private property in order to make an arrest.

Amendment 5.

No person shall be held to answer for a capital [punishable by death] **or otherwise infamous crime** [an "otherwise infamous crime" is one which is punishable by imprisonment or death] **unless on a presentment or indictment of a grand jury** [a grand jury is a jury that investigates allegations of a crime and issues indictments if it finds there is sufficient evidence against the person or persons. An indictment is a formal written charge against one or more people and presented to a court. A presentment is a report made by a grand jury of an offence that the grand jury observed or learned during their investigations.]**, except in cases arising in the land or naval forces, or in the militia, when in actual service, in time of war or public danger; nor shall any person be subject for the same offence to be twice put in jeopardy of life or limb** [this means that each person has the right to be permanently free from further prosecution of a crime after the trial for that crime and any appeals from that decision are completed]**; nor shall be**

compelled in any criminal case to be a witness against himself, nor be deprived of life, liberty, or property, without due process of law ["due process of law" refers to the regular administration or course of the law]; nor shall private property be taken for public use without just compensation.

That a person cannot "be deprived of life, liberty, or property, without due process of law" says that, without following the guidelines of the law, these things cannot be tampered with by an all-powerful government.

Amendment 6.

In all criminal prosecutions, the accused shall enjoy [have, possess and use with satisfaction] the right to a speedy and public trial, by an impartial jury of the state and district wherein the crime shall have been committed, which district shall have been previously ascertained by law, and to be informed of the nature and cause of the accusation; to be confronted with the witnesses against him; to have compulsory process [a legal document ordering a person to appear in court] for obtaining witnesses in his favor, and to have the assistance of counsel for his defense.

The right to a "speedy and public trial" was written into the Constitution because earlier in Great Britain people were sometimes held in prison for years without trial and then, finally, given a trial held in secret.

Amendment 7.

In suits at common law ["at common law" means according to common law: that body of rules, principles and customs which have been received from our ancestors, and recognized by courts. It is different from "statutory law," which is laws made by legislatures. It applies to disputes between private parties in non-criminal matters], **where the value in controversy shall exceed twenty dollars, the right of trial by jury shall be preserved, and no fact tried by a jury shall be otherwise re-examined in any court of the United States than according to the rules of the common law.**

This amendment concerns lawsuits in federal courts, but the state courts also have jury trials as covered by their own constitutions.

Amendment 8.

Excessive bail [money given to allow the temporary release of a person from jail and to guarantee the person will return at a certain date. If the person fails to return, the money is given up.] **shall not be required, nor excessive fines imposed, nor cruel and unusual punishments inflicted.**

In Great Britain, high treason could be punished by hanging a person by the neck, cutting him down and then disemboweling him while he was still living, then cutting off his head and cutting the body into four parts. Great Britain outlawed this punishment in 1814. Other English punishments included cutting off the ears, slitting the nose and branding on the cheek. The Eighth Amendment forbade such "cruel and unusual" punishment in the United States.

Amendment 9.

The enumeration [to mention items one by one] **in the Constitution of certain rights shall not be construed** [interpreted or explained] **to deny or disparage** [discredit or belittle] **others retained by the people.**

During Congress' debates concerning the Bill of Rights, there were members who argued that if some of the rights to be protected were named, it could be interpreted as meaning that other rights not so named were not to be protected.

James Madison led the Congress in adopting the Bill of Rights. In his speech of June 8, 1789, where he introduced the Bill, he stated:

"It has been objected also against a bill of rights, that, by enumerating particular exceptions to the grant of power, it would disparage those rights which were not placed in that enumeration; and it might follow by implication, that those rights which were not singled out, were intended to be assigned into the hands of the General Government, and were consequently insecure. This is one of the most plausible arguments I have ever heard urged against the admission of a bill of rights into this system; but, I conceive, that it may be guarded against. I have attempted it, as gentlemen may see by turning to [here Madison refers to the next paragraph given below, which is also from Madison's speech on June 8, 1789]."

"The exceptions here or elsewhere in the Constitution, made in favor of particular rights, shall not be so construed as to diminish the just importance of other rights retained by the people, or as to enlarge the powers delegated by the Constitution; but either as actual limitations of such powers, or as inserted merely for greater caution."

Amendment 10.

The powers not delegated to the United States by the Constitution, nor prohibited by it to the states, are reserved to the states respectively, or to the people.

The powers not given to the U.S. federal government, or the powers not denied to the states by the Constitution, are the powers of the states or the people. This makes clear that the federal government cannot take away the power of the states or the people. For example, the states have power over marriages and divorces; the states can pass their own laws; the states can collect money from taxes; etc.

Amendment 11.

The judicial power of the United States shall not be construed to extend to any suit in law or equity, commenced or prosecuted against one of the United States, by citizens of another state, or by citizens or subjects of any foreign state.

The Eleventh Amendment was adopted in 1795.

"The judicial power of the United States" refers to the power of the U.S. federal courts. This amendment says a citizen of one state may not sue another state in federal court, but must sue in state court. However, a citizen of one state may sue state authorities in federal court for depriving them of their Constitutional rights.

In a 1793 court case, a South Carolina man sued the state of Georgia over an inheritance. This case went to the U.S. Supreme Court where the State of Georgia argued that it could not be sued in a federal court. The Supreme Court ruled, however, that it could be sued in a federal court. After this case, the State of Georgia led a movement to adopt this amendment, as many states, under great financial hardship, felt alarmed by this 1793 Supreme Court ruling.

Amendment 12.

The Constitution states how the president and vice president shall be elected by the electoral college, but does not tell us how the candidates are selected. This procedure evolved over time. By the early 1800s, two major political parties dominated the elections. Here, "party" means a political organization. Today, the two main parties, Republicans and Democrats, dominate the political scene, although other smaller political parties contend for attention.

In the first part of an election year, most states conduct primary elections to choose candidates. The word "primary" means first. These elections occur first, followed by the election where the final choice is made for the political office.

All registered voters are allowed to vote in primary elections. Most states hold what are called "closed primaries," where the voter may only vote for the candidates of the political party to which he belongs. For example, a Republican can only vote for Republican candidates. Some states hold "open primaries," where voters may vote for candidates of whatever political party, but may only vote for one candidate for president and one for vice president.

Some states do not hold primary elections, but hold what are called "caucuses," which are meetings of members of a political party.

The winners of the primary elections and caucuses in each state send delegates to their party's national convention. A delegate is someone chosen to represent or act on behalf of another person or organization.

The process of selecting the candidates for president and vice president culminates in the separate Republican and Democratic national conventions, as well as conventions for the smaller political parties, where the delegates selected by primaries and caucuses select who will be their party's candidates.

Then, in November, at the presidential election, called the "general election," U.S. citizens vote for the candidates of their choice.

However, an additional step remains to electing the president after the general election. That is the Electoral College.

In most states the winning party sends electors to the Electoral College to vote for their party's candidates for president and vice president. Each state sends as many electors to the Electoral College as it has U.S. senators and representatives. Two states allow electors to be split between the parties. Since the appointment of the electors is governed by state law the details of this procedure vary from state to state.

The Constitution has no provision to prevent electors from voting for a candidate other than the one they pledged to vote for. The electors, bound only by their pledge, have, in a few instances, voted for someone else.

The first Monday after the second Wednesday in December the electors [in this case, electors are the people who vote at the Electoral College] "meet" to vote for the president and vice president—the Electoral College never actually meets as a single group. Instead, the electors from each individual state meet in their own state capitals and cast their votes which are sent to the U.S. Congress for a final count.

On January 6, both the House of Representatives and the Senate, sitting together, count the electoral votes and then officially name the president and vice president.

Today, thanks to voting machines, radio, television and computers, we know the outcome of an election within a few hours of its completion. The vote of the Electoral College, for all practical purposes, has become a formality, since results can easily be predicted immediately after the general election (which candidate won in each state and how many electoral votes each candidate will receive).

The electors shall meet in their respective states, and vote by ballot for president and vice president, one of whom at least shall not be an inhabitant of the same state with themselves [at least one of the persons the elector votes for to be president or vice president must be from a different state than the elector]; **they shall name in their ballots the person voted for as president, and in distinct** [separate] **ballots the person voted for as vice president, and they shall make distinct lists of all persons voted for as president, and of all persons voted for as vice president, and of the number of votes for each, which lists they shall sign and certify, and transmit sealed to the seat of the government of the United States, directed to the president of the Senate; the president of the Senate shall, in the presence of the Senate and House of Representatives, open all the certificates, and the votes shall then be counted; the person having the greatest number of votes for president shall be the president, if such number be a majority of the whole number of electors appointed; and if no person have such majority, then from the persons having**

the highest numbers not exceeding three on the list of those voted for as president, the House of Representatives shall choose immediately, by ballot, the president. But in choosing the president, the votes shall be taken by states, the representation from each state having one vote; a quorum for this purpose shall consist of a member or members from two-thirds of the states, and a majority of all the states shall be necessary to a choice. And if the House of Representatives shall not choose a president whenever the right of choice shall devolve upon them, before the fourth day of March next following, then the vice president shall act as president, as in the case of the death or other constitutional disability of the president. [The Twentieth Amendment superseded the preceding sentence.] The person having the greatest number of votes as vice president shall be the vice president, if such number be a majority of the whole number of electors appointed, and if no person have a majority, then from the two highest numbers on the list the Senate shall choose the vice president; a quorum for the purpose shall consist of two-thirds of the whole number of senators, and a majority of the whole number shall be necessary to a choice. But no person constitutionally ineligible to the office of president shall be eligible to that of vice president of the United States.

The Twelfth Amendment was adopted in 1804.

Prior to this amendment, the electors each cast two votes at the Electoral College—the person getting the most votes became president and the one with the second highest became vice president. In the presidential election of 1800, Thomas Jefferson, the presidential candidate and Aaron Burr, the vice presidential candidate, each received the same number of electoral votes. The House of Representatives had to decide which person of this tie became president and which vice president. Jefferson was elected president. This amendment changed the Electoral College system so that electors needed to vote once for the president and once for the vice president. Currently, when a political party nominates a presidential candidate, that candidate chooses a "running mate" to be vice presidential candidate. Both appear on the presidential ballot together and the people vote for them together. The Electoral College, however, votes separately for president and vice president.

Over the years, people have put proposals forward to eliminate the Electoral College and simply choose the president via a direct election by the people. These proposals have not gained enough support to get passed.

Amendment 13.

Section 1. Neither slavery nor involuntary servitude [a slave-like condition. Sometimes British criminals were sold to American colonists to labor for them during the term of their sentence.]**, except as a punishment for crime whereof the party shall have been duly convicted, shall exist within the United States, or any place subject to their jurisdiction.**

Section 2. Congress shall have power to enforce this article by appropriate legislation.

The Thirteenth Amendment was adopted in 1865.

The United States Civil War between the northern and southern states was fought between 1861 and 1865. During that time, the president of the U.S. declared the slaves free. However, some legal questions arose about the president's authority to issue such a declaration, so this amendment was adopted.

Amendment 14.

Section 1. All persons born or naturalized [citizenship given to a person born in another country] **in the United States, and subject to the jurisdiction thereof, are citizens of the United States and of the state wherein they reside. No**

state shall make or enforce any law which shall abridge the privileges or immunities [freedoms] of citizens of the United States; nor shall any state deprive any person of life, liberty, or property without due process of law; nor deny to any person within its jurisdiction the equal protection of the laws.

Abolishing slavery with the Thirteenth Amendment did not give the freed slaves all their rights. For example, towns in some states did not allow former slaves to appear other than as servants. This section of Amendment 14 gave each person born in the United States, or naturalized as a U.S. citizen, the rights of citizenship and protection under the law.

Based on the Fifth Amendment and the Fourteenth Amendment's direction that "No state shall deny to any person who lives within its jurisdiction the equal protection of the laws," the courts have developed rules whereby most of the federal Bill of Rights now applies to state governments as well. Also, based on this the courts look closely at race, religion, national origin, gender and age as key categories for protection against discrimination.

Section 2. Representatives shall be apportioned among the several states according to their respective numbers, counting the whole number of persons in each state, excluding Indians not taxed. But when the right to vote at

any election for the choice of electors for president and vice president of the United States, representatives in Congress, the executive and judicial officers of a state, or the members of the legislature thereof, is denied to any of the male inhabitants of such state, being twenty-one years of age, and citizens of the United States, or in any way abridged, except for participation in rebellion or other crime, the basis of representation therein shall be reduced in the proportion which the number of such male citizens shall bear to the whole number of male citizens twenty-one years of age in such state.

This section penalized states which had not allowed former male slaves to vote in federal elections. The penalty was a reduction in the number of representatives a state could have in the House of Representatives. This penalty was never used. This section was later modified by the Nineteenth Amendment, which gave women the right to vote, and the Twenty-Sixth Amendment, which gave eighteen-year-olds the right to vote.

Section 3. No person shall be a senator or representative in Congress, or elector of president and vice president, or hold any office, civil or military, under the United States, or under any state, who, having previously taken an oath, as a member of Congress, or as an officer of the United States, or as a member of any state legislature, or as an executive or judicial officer of any state, to support the Constitution of the United States, shall have engaged in insurrection or rebellion against the same, or given aid or comfort to the enemies thereof. But Congress may, by vote of two-thirds of each House, remove such disability.

Section 3 prevented persons who had taken an oath to support the Constitution and then fought against the United States during the Civil War to hold governmental offices without approval from Congress.

Section 4. The validity of the public debt of the United States, authorized by law, including debts incurred for payment of pensions and bounties [rewards offered to people by the government for performing certain acts. During the Civil War, a cash bounty was offered for enlisting in the army.] for services in suppressing insurrection or rebellion, shall not be questioned. But neither the United States nor any state shall assume or pay any debt or obligation incurred in aid of insurrection or rebellion against the United States, or any claim for the loss or emancipation [the action of freeing from slavery] of any slave; but all such debts, obligations, and claims shall be held illegal and void.

All debts incurred by the United States during the Civil War were to be paid. But no debts of the southern states that tried to withdraw from the United States could be paid, as such debts were considered illegal and void. After the war, the southern states owed more than $1.4 billion to their own citizens, as well as to Great Britain, France and other countries. This amendment prohibited the federal government from paying back that money. No payment could be given to former slave owners for their former slaves.

Section 5. The Congress shall have the power to enforce, by appropriate legislation, the provisions of this article.

The Fourteenth Amendment was adopted in 1868.

Amendment 15.

Section 1. The right of citizens of the United States to vote shall not be denied or abridged by the United States or by any state on account of race, color, or previous condition of servitude.

It thus became illegal to disallow former slaves to vote because of their race, color or having previously been a slave.

Section 2. The Congress shall have the power to enforce this article by appropriate legislation.

The Fifteenth Amendment was adopted in 1870.

Amendment 16.

The Congress shall have power to lay and collect taxes on incomes, from whatever source derived, without apportionment among the several States, and without regard to any census or enumeration.

The Sixteenth Amendment was adopted in 1913.

This amendment allowed the Congress to set up the income tax. In 1913 when the income tax started, the American people were promised that the income tax would be temporary, perhaps limited to times of war and would not represent a threat to their liberties.

In 1913, the average family paid approximately 1% of their yearly family income in taxes. The very rich, who had incomes over $500,000 per year, paid 6% of their incomes in income tax.

By 1950, the average American family of four members paid approximately 2% of their yearly income in income taxes.

Today, the federal tax rates are much higher. The highest tax rates go as high as 35% for individuals and 39% for corporations.

Amendment 17.

Prior to the Seventeenth Amendment, U.S. senators were elected by the state legislatures. After this amendment was ratified, the people of each state, not the legislatures, elected the senators. This amendment uses the word "electors," and here the word refers to people who vote in elections for U.S. senators and state legislators, namely citizens of the state. In that each state establishes its own voter qualifications, this amendment allows that anyone deemed qualified to vote for "the most numerous branch of the state legislature" (meaning the State House of Representatives, or the State Assembly, or the State House of Delegates as it is sometimes called) is also eligible to vote for their state's U.S. Senators.

The Senate of the United States shall be composed of two senators from each state, elected by the people thereof for six years; and each senator shall have one vote. The electors in each state shall have the qualifications requisite for electors of the most numerous branch of the state legislatures.

When vacancies happen in the representation of any state in the senate, the executive authority [governor] **of such state shall issue writs of election** [formal written documents ordering elections] **to fill such vacancies:** *Provided* ["provided" is used in legal documents to introduce a condition or requirement], **That the legislature of any state may empower the executive thereof to make temporary appointments until the people fill the vacancies by election as the legislature may direct.**

This amendment shall not be so construed as to affect the election or term of any senator chosen before it becomes valid as part of the Constitution.

The Seventeenth Amendment was adopted in 1913.

Amendment 18.

This amendment made it illegal to make, sell or transport liquor. It was repealed by the Twenty-first Amendment in 1933.

Section 1. After one year from the ratification of this article the manufacture, sale, or transportation of intoxicating liquors within, the importation thereof into, or the exportation thereof from the United States and all territory subject to the jurisdiction thereof for beverage purposes is hereby prohibited.

Section 2. The Congress and the several states shall have concurrent [existing at the same time] **power to enforce this article by appropriate legislation.**

Section 3. This article shall be inoperative unless it shall

have been ratified as an amendment to the Constitution by the legislatures of the several states, as provided in the Constitution, within seven years from the date of the submission hereof to the states by the Congress.

The Eighteenth Amendment was proposed by Congress in 1917, and adopted by the states in 1919. One year later, in 1920, it went into effect.

Amendment 19.

The right of citizens of the United States to vote shall not be denied or abridged by the United States or by any state on account of sex.

Congress shall have power to enforce this article by appropriate legislation.

The Nineteenth Amendment was adopted in 1920.

The Nineteenth Amendment gave women the right to vote.

Amendment 20.

Section 1. The terms of the president and vice president shall end at noon on the 20th day of January, and the terms of senators and representatives at noon on the third day of January, of the years in which such terms would have

ended if this article had not been ratified; and the terms of their successors shall then begin.

Prior to this amendment, the president and U.S. senators and representatives were elected in November, but they wouldn't take office until March of the following year. This Amendment allowed Congress to start work on January 3, and the president to begin work on January 20, rather than in March.

Section 2. The Congress shall assemble at least once in every year, and such meeting shall begin at noon on the third day of January, unless they shall by law appoint a different day.

Originally, the Constitution provided that Congress start on "the first Monday in December," and this section changed it to January 3.

Section 3. If, at the time fixed for the beginning of the term of the president, the president elect shall have died, the vice president elect shall become president. If a president shall not have been chosen before the time fixed for the beginning of his term, of if the president elect shall have failed to qualify, then the vice president elect shall act as president until a president shall have qualified; and the Congress may by law provide for the case wherein neither a president elect nor a vice president shall have qualified, declaring who shall then act as president, or the manner in which one who is to act shall be selected, and such person shall act accordingly until a president or vice president shall have qualified.

The Twelfth Amendment did not cover the possibility of the president elect dying before taking office, so this gave Congress the power to determine who should act temporarily as president.

Section 4. The Congress may by law provide for the case of the death of any of the persons from whom the House of Representatives may choose a president whenever the right of choice shall have devolved upon them, and for the case of the death of any of the persons from whom the Senate may choose a vice president whenever the right of choice shall have devolved upon them.

Section 5. Sections 1 and 2 shall take effect on the 15th day of October following the ratification of this article.

Section 6. This article shall be inoperative unless it shall have been ratified as an amendment to the Constitution by the legislatures of three-fourths of the several states within seven years from the date of its submission.

The Twentieth Amendment was adopted in 1933.

Amendment 21.

Section 1. The eighteenth article of amendment to the Constitution of the United States is hereby repealed.

Section 2. The transportation or importation into any state, territory, or possession of the United States for delivery or use therein of intoxicating liquors, in violation of the laws thereof, is hereby prohibited.

This amendment returned to the States the right to have alcoholic beverages and the right not to have them. Each State could pass their own laws regarding alcohol.

Section 3. This article shall be inoperative unless it shall have been ratified as an amendment to the Constitution by conventions in the several states, as provided in the Constitution, within seven years from the date of the submission hereof to the states by the Congress.

The Twenty-first Amendment was adopted in 1933.

Amendment 22.

Section 1. No person shall be elected to the office of the president more than twice, and no person who has held the office of president, or acted as president, for more than two years of a term to which some other person was elected

president shall be elected to the office of the president more than once. But this article shall not apply to any person holding the office of president when this article was proposed by the Congress, and shall not prevent any person who may be holding the office of president, or acting as president, during the term within which this article becomes operative from holding the office of president or acting as president during the remainder of such term.

Section 2. This article shall be inoperative unless it shall have been ratified as an amendment to the Constitution by the legislatures of three-fourths of the several states within seven years from the date of its submission to the states by the Congress.

The Twenty-second Amendment was adopted in 1951.

Franklin D. Roosevelt was president of the U.S. from 1933 until his death in 1945. He was elected to four four-year terms as president. This amendment limits the number of four-year terms a president can hold to two.

Amendment 23.

Section 1. The district [area of a country or city] constituting [forming] the seat of government of the United States shall appoint in such manner as Congress may direct:

A number of electors of president and vice president equal to the whole number of senators and representatives in Congress to which the district would be entitled if it were a state, but in no event more than the least populous state; they shall be in addition to those appointed by the states, but they shall be considered, for the purposes of the election of president and vice president, to be electors appointed by a state; and they shall meet in the district and perform such duties as provided by the twelfth article of amendment.

Section 2. The Congress shall have power to enforce this article by appropriate legislation.

The Twenty-third Amendment was adopted in 1961.

Prior to this amendment, citizens living in the District of Columbia could not vote in presidential elections. This resulted from the District of Columbia not being a state and, therefore, not eligible for electors. This amendment allowed such citizens to vote and granted electors to the district in presidential elections.

Amendment 24.

Section 1. The right of citizens of the United States to vote in any primary [an election where members of a political party choose their candidates. The word "primary" means first. This election occurs first, followed by the election where the final choice of political office is made.] **or other election for president or vice president, for electors for president or vice president, or for senator or representative in Congress, shall not be denied or abridged by the United States or any state by reason of failure to pay poll tax** [in this use "poll" means a person's "head." A poll tax is a tax per "head" or a tax on each person collected before each may vote.] **or other tax.**

Section 2. The Congress shall have power to enforce this article by appropriate legislation.

The Twenty-fourth Amendment was adopted in 1964.

No citizen can be denied the right to vote in presidential or congressional elections by reason of not paying a poll tax or other taxes. Some states collected such taxes to keep African-Americans and poor people from voting.

Amendment 25.

Section 1. In case of the removal of the president from office or of his death or resignation, the vice president shall become president.

Section 2. Whenever there is a vacancy in the office of the vice president, the president shall nominate a vice president

who shall take office upon confirmation by a majority vote of both houses of Congress.

Prior to this amendment, when a vacancy occurred in the office of the vice president, it remained vacant until the next election.

Section 3. Whenever the president transmits to the president pro tempore of the Senate and the Speaker of the House of Representatives his written declaration that he is unable to discharge the powers and duties of his office, and until he transmits to them a written declaration to the contrary, such powers and duties shall be discharged by the vice president as acting president.

If the president informs the leaders in the Senate and House that he is unable to perform his duties, the vice president performs the duties of president until the president informs such leaders he is again capable of performing his duties.

Section 4. Whenever the vice president and a majority of either the principal officers of the executive departments [Currently there are fifteen executive departments, such as the Departments of Agriculture, Commerce and Defense. The principal officers of these departments are called Secretaries and, along with the vice president, make up the president's "cabinet" or group of advisors.] **or of such other body as Congress may by law provide, transmit to the president pro tempore of the Senate and the Speaker of the House of Representatives their written declaration that the president is unable to discharge the powers and duties of his office, the vice president shall immediately assume the powers and duties of the office as acting president.**

Thereafter, when the president transmits to the president pro tempore of the Senate and the Speaker of the House of Representatives his written declaration that no inability exists, he shall resume the powers and duties of his office unless the vice president and a majority of either the principal officers of the executive department or of such other body as Congress may by law provide, transmit within four days to the president pro tempore of the Senate and the Speaker of the House of Representatives their written declaration that the president is unable to discharge the powers and duties of his office. Thereupon Congress shall decide the issue, assembling within forty-eight hours for that purpose if not in session. If the Congress, within twenty-one days after receipt of the latter written declaration, or, if Congress is not in session, within twenty-one days after Congress is required to assemble, determines by two-thirds vote of both houses that the president is unable to discharge

the powers and duties of his office, the vice president shall continue to discharge the same as acting president; otherwise, the president shall resume the powers and duties of his office.

The Twenty-fifth Amendment was adopted in 1967.

The Twenty-fifth Amendment was passed to lay out what was to happen if the president became unable to perform the duties of the president. President Kennedy's assassination in 1963 prompted this.

Amendment 26.

Section 1. The right of citizens of the United States, who are eighteen years of age or older, to vote shall not be denied or abridged by the United States or by any state on account of age.

Section 2. The Congress shall have power to enforce this article by appropriate legislation.

The Twenty-sixth Amendment was adopted in 1971.

Amendment 27.

No law, varying the compensation for the services of the senators and representatives, shall take effect, until an election of representatives shall have intervened.

The Twenty-seventh Amendment was adopted in 1992.

Passed by Congress in 1789, this amendment was not ratified by three-fourths of the states until 1992. If senators and representatives approve a pay raise for themselves it may not take effect until after an election of representatives, which occurs every two years. This gives the citizens the opportunity to express their opinion of the pay raise at the voting booth before the raise takes effect.

Applying the Constitution

The U.S. Constitution is a relatively short document, in its original form consisting of only four handwritten pages. As such, the executive, judicial and legislative branches of our government developed laws and official rules to apply it.

The right of habeas corpus;
Article 1, Section 9

When a person or group challenges the actions of the legislature or the executive branch of our government because they believe such actions are unjust or incorrect according to the Constitution, the role of interpreting the Constitution is given to and assumed by the Supreme Court.

Over the last two hundred years, many Supreme Court decisions have explained how the Constitution should be applied, and these have been described in numerous publications. Many new and conflicting ideas regarding our Constitution have been forwarded by all segments of society. As new Supreme Court justices are appointed to the court, as our society changes and other factors intervene, some decisions of the Supreme Court have been changed over time or, it is said, the Court "reversed itself." When a court "reverses itself," it has essentially changed its mind. First, it decides that some issue should be decided one way and then, when it reverses itself, it rules that the issue should be decided another way.

The purpose of this book so far has been to provide a brief background on how and why the Constitution was written, and then to present the actual Constitution with explanatory commentary. All citizens have a duty to understand this original document, the supreme law of our land. Further study can then make sense as an individual sees how various interpretations of the Constitution have emerged and what these interpretations actually mean. All citizens have the power and choice to ask questions or write letters to presidential and congressional candidates and vote for those candidates they believe will ensure the correct application of our Constitution.

A thorough study of how our Constitution has been interpreted over its history and how it is interpreted today would go beyond the scope of this book. However, we will briefly examine this aspect.

One must remember that the Supreme Court has dealt with an enormous number of cases, many of which are extremely lengthy in themselves. Additionally, tremendous amounts of material has been written about them. Some decisions of the Supreme Court run well over 100 pages in length. The entire texts of all Supreme Court decisions are published yearly. These books covering all Supreme Court decisions and comments about them stretch well over seventy-five feet on bookshelves.

To really understand the workings of politics, our government and how the Constitution has been applied, one must understand that individual men and women make the decisions of government. The ways they are supposed to make such decisions are laid out in the Constitution. How they follow the basic constitutional principles determines whether their decisions either forward or hinder, protect or undermine our rights and freedoms as described in our Constitution.

Our Changing Government

The Constitution allows for amendments and new laws based on the Constitution so that we are able to adapt to meet the changing needs of the future. Here are a few examples of changes that, almost everyone would agree, are based on the fundamental principles and values expressed in the Constitution:

When the Constitution was ratified in 1788, the United States had a government that was established by and run by white males who owned property. Women, African-Americans and Indians were not allowed to vote. It was not until the 1820s and 1830s that individual states dropped the qualifications of owning property in order to vote or hold a governmental office. It was not until the 1870 passage of the Fifteenth Amendment that African-Americans and Indians were allowed to vote, and the 1920 passage of the Nineteenth Amendment that women were allowed to vote.

We see that when Constitutional principles are applied to meet new challenges the country prospers. When they are disregarded, individual rights and prosperity diminish and new problems arise. Thomas Jefferson spoke about sticking to basic principles in his first presidential speech in 1801:

"**Equal and exact justice to all men, of whatever state or persuasion** [belief], **religious or political; peace, commerce, and honest friendship with all nations**—**entangling** [involving in difficulties or complicated circumstances that are difficult to get out of] **alliances with none... freedom of religion; freedom of the press; freedom of person under the protection of the habeas corpus; and trial by juries impartially selected**—**these principles form the bright constellation** [a group of stars that form a recognizable pattern] **which has gone before us, and guided our steps through an age of revolution and reformation** [the correction of anything corrupt]. **The wisdom of our sages** [wise people] **and the blood of our heroes have** been devoted to their attainment. They should be the creed [set of beliefs or aims that guide someone's actions] of our political faith—the text of civil instruction—the touchstone [any test or criteria by which the qualities of a thing are tried] by which to try [test or examine] the services of those we trust; and should we wander from them in moments of error or alarm, let us hasten to retrace our steps and to regain the road which alone leads to peace, liberty, and safety."

Our ability to follow Jefferson's advice begins with our familiarity with the Constitution, but our success depends upon each individual's willingness to participate in government. The government is responsible to the people and will be as long as the people do not give up their right and responsibility to inform and direct the actions of their government. Whether it is through voting, writing to your representative, starting a petition or by exercising any of the other rights guaranteed by the Constitution, it is the actions of you and me and our fellow citizens that determine whether our government changes in ways that lead us toward the goals stated in the preamble or away from them.

Legal Precedents

"Precede" means to "go before." The word "precedent" means a legal decision that serves as an example, reason or justification for a later one.

The law in England developed from the decisions handed down by the English courts. Earlier decisions formed precedents upon which later decisions were based, when the later cases were similar in some respect to the earlier decisions.

The early American colonists brought this aspect of English law with them. This system then became part of the law in the Colonies and later in the United States.

When the Supreme Court makes a decision, it becomes a precedent, which must be followed by all other state and federal courts. The Supreme Court usually follows precedents set by earlier Supreme Court decisions, but does not need to do so.

For example, the Supreme Court may decide a case concerning fishermen, based upon a precedent of an earlier case concerning fishermen, and give a similar ruling.

Or it may state that the current case concerning fisherman is different from earlier precedents regarding fishermen and make its decision based upon different precedents—for example, precedents concerning ships or commerce.

Or it may simply ignore the earlier precedent concerning fishermen and make a decision different from the precedent.

Or it may overrule the earlier precedent concerning fishermen and rule that the precedent was a wrong decision and make a new, different decision.

Or it may rule that an issue should be dealt with by Congress making a new law to resolve it or by the president applying an existing law, and refer the matter back to Congress or the president.

For the thirty-five years from 1953 through 1988, the Supreme Court overruled eighty previous Supreme Court precedents. It declared unconstitutional 356 state laws and 55 acts of the U.S. Congress.

Whatever the Supreme Court decides becomes the law of the land.

Cases at the Supreme Court

Most of the cases that the Supreme Court hears are requests that a higher court decide a matter from either state courts (which decide matters based on laws of individual states) or federal courts (which decide matters based on laws of the United States). The cases from state courts are first reviewed by the highest court in that state. The cases from federal courts are first reviewed by the court of appeals. If the losing party from one of these state or federal court cases wants the case reviewed by the Supreme Court, that party must petition the Supreme Court. Less than one or two percent of these petitions are accepted.

Usually, federal courts decide only "federal questions"—matters that relate to the meaning of a law passed by the U.S.

Congress, a treaty between a foreign country and the U.S., or the Constitution itself. As disputes about property, contracts or personal injury usually do not deal in such issues and are based on state law, such matters are tried in state courts.

Federal courts and the Supreme Court may not hear a case unless it is a federal question. Article III, Section 2 of the Constitution defines this mainly as "all cases... arising under this Constitution, the laws of the United States, and treaties."

A party petitioning the Supreme Court to hear a particular case must show to the satisfaction of the Supreme Court that the case involves a constitutional question, a law of the U.S. Congress or the administration of such a law, or a treaty of the U.S. The Constitution also allows federal courts and the Supreme Court to hear cases where the United States itself is a party, disputes between states, disputes arising from actions out at sea, cases involving foreign diplomats, and those between persons living in different states. The Supreme Court's most important function is to ensure the Constitution is being applied and upheld, whether the case involves a law passed by the U.S. Congress or the Constitution itself.

The nine justices on the Supreme Court look over the petitions filed for cases to be heard by the Supreme Court and pick which ones they want to hear. Four of the nine justices must agree to hear a case before the Supreme Court accepts it. The usual reasons for acceptance of a case are that it involves fundamental Constitutional questions, an issue of general importance to the United States or its citizens, rights of citizens, a federal law that has not yet been interpreted by the Court, or previous decisions by federal or state courts that conflict on an issue involving federal matters.

If the Supreme Court accepts a case, the justices review the records of the case from the lower courts, study the legal papers presented by the attorneys for both sides, and hear oral arguments. Then a majority vote by the justices determines the outcome. The most senior Supreme Court justice who voted with the majority assigns a justice to write an opinion, and that opinion becomes the new precedent upon which similar cases must be decided in all lower courts. If a justice disagrees with the majority opinion, that justice may write a dissenting opinion, but it does not set a precedent.

Supreme Court Justices

Supreme Court justices are chosen by the president and confirmed by a majority vote in the Senate. The most common reason the Senate fails to confirm a Supreme Court nominee is political. For example, a president of one political party may have difficulty getting his nominee confirmed by the Senate if senators of another political party control the Senate.

Supreme Court justices hold their offices for life or until they retire. The Constitution states they may be removed from office by the impeachment process, but no Supreme Court justice has been removed.

Since they want their policies to extend beyond their term in office, presidents usually select nominees for Supreme Court justices whose views on government policy mirror their own. The main reason, then, why the Supreme Court changes direction over time is that new presidents appoint justices with views similar to their own.

Supreme Court Decisions

Court cases are named such as *Jones v. Smith* (1880), with the plaintiff's name given first. The plaintiff is the person who brings a lawsuit into a court of law or the person who makes the formal charge or complaint. The "v." stands for versus, which means that one person or group is in contest with another person or group. The second name cites the defendant who is the person or group who is being sued or the person defending himself or itself against the plaintiff. The names of court cases are usually italicized. The date after the name of the case shows the year it was decided.

The Supreme Court interprets the Constitution and its rulings and interpretations become law. Only a new Constitutional amendment can override its decisions, and this has happened only a few times. Here are three examples of the Supreme Court interpreting the Constitution.

Dred Scott v. Sandford

Dred Scott v. Sandford (1857). In 1820, the U.S. Congress passed a law called the "Missouri Compromise," which excluded slavery from any state formed from the lands purchased from France in the Louisiana Purchase in 1803, except Missouri. It included the land west of the Mississippi River to the Rocky Mountains, and from the Gulf of Mexico to Canada.

Per this law, Missouri was to be a "slave state," or one in which slavery was legal when Missouri joined the United States as a state in 1821. Other states that were to join the United States from the Louisiana Territory were to be "free states," or ones in which slavery was illegal.

Dred Scott was an African-American slave who was owned by a white man in Missouri. In 1836 Scott was taken by his owner to a territory of the U.S., now the state of Minnesota, where slavery was expressly forbidden. In 1846 Scott brought suit in the Missouri state court on the grounds that his having lived in the "free" territory of Minnesota released him from slavery. The Missouri Supreme Court ruled that because Scott was brought back to the state of Missouri, where slavery was legal, this act still made him a slave. This case went to the Supreme Court, where it was decided in 1857 that the United States government had no power to make African-Americans citizens, whether they were free or slaves, because when the Constitution was ratified, African-Americans could not be citizens of the United States. Accordingly, the Supreme Court ruled that Scott was still a slave.

The *Dred Scott* decision went on to state the Missouri Compromise was in violation of the Constitution and that Congress could not prohibit slavery in territories of the United States. This case brought about much bitterness in the United States and widened the breach between the Northern and Southern States and was one of the causes of the American Civil War.

The Fourteenth Amendment to the Constitution in 1868, which gave African-Americans the right to citizenship, reversed the 1857 *Dred Scott* decision, which held that African-Americans were not American citizens.

Pollock v. Farmers' Loan and Trust Co.

Pollock v. Farmers' Loan and Trust Co. (1895). Our federal tax system of today is relatively new. From 1789, when the Constitution was ratified, until 1909, the federal government depended mainly on excise taxes (which are taxes on the manufacture, sale or consumption of various commodities within a country, such as tobacco, airline tickets, gasoline, liquor, etc.) and customs taxes (which are taxes charged on goods imported from other countries) for its revenues. The corporate income tax was started in 1909. Only since 1913 have we had the individual income tax.

Taxation has always been a heated issue in American politics, since before independence from Great Britain to the present. In 1819, in a famous Supreme Court decision, Chief Justice John Marshall stated, "the power to tax involves the power to destroy."

During the Civil War, from 1862 through 1871, an income tax helped to meet the demands of financing the war. Then, in 1894, an income tax was again established, but it was declared unconstitutional by the Supreme Court in *Pollock v. Farmers' Loan and Trust Co.* (1895) since the income tax is a "direct tax."

A "direct tax" is a tax laid directly on the person who is going to pay it, such as an income tax or a property tax. An "indirect tax" is a tax on manufactured goods, imports, etc. that is paid "indirectly" by the consumer because it is included in the price.

The 1894 Income Tax Law set up taxes on the rent or income derived from land. However, the tax on the income from land was not divided among the states according to their population (apportioned) because the value of the income varied from state to state and had no relationship to the number of people. Article I, Section 2 includes the clause "direct taxes shall be apportioned among the several states which may be included within this Union, according to their respective numbers." This means no state shall have its citizens taxed at a higher rate than any other state by the federal government in proportion to their populations. Also, Article I, Section 9 similarly states, "No capitation [a tax or fee of the same amount for every person], or other direct tax, shall be laid, unless in proportion to the census..."

The Court in the *Pollock* case declared that the tax on income from land was actually a tax on the land itself, and therefore such an income tax was a "direct tax" which should have been apportioned according to the Constitution. As such, it declared the 1894 Income Tax Law unconstitutional.

The Sixteenth Amendment in 1913 made the income tax legal, even though such a tax is in violation of Article I, Sections 2 and 9, and overturned the *Pollock* decision.

Oregon v. Mitchell

In the *Oregon v. Mitchell* (1970) case the Supreme Court ruled that eighteen-year-olds could vote in federal elections, but not in state and local elections. A year later in 1971, the Twenty-sixth Amendment gave eighteen-year-olds the right to vote in all elections, thereby overturning the portion of the *Oregon v. Mitchell* decision which denied them voting rights in state and local elections.

Responsibility of the Supreme Court

The ultimate responsibility of the Supreme Court is to protect constitutional rights and liberties. Many examples of what government may not do are given in the Constitution:

– The privilege of writ of habeas corpus shall not be suspended unless the public safety may require it

– No ex post facto law shall be passed

– No tax may be collected on articles imported from another state

– No direct tax shall be collected unless in proportion to a census (this was changed by the Sixteenth Amendment, which allowed an income tax)

– No money shall be drawn from the Treasury without appropriations made by law

– No title of nobility shall be granted

– Congress shall make no law respecting the establishment of religion; prohibiting the free exercise of religion; abridging the freedom of speech, or the press, or the right of people to peaceably assemble, or the right to petition the government for correction of wrongs.

The Constitution set up a system of government that limits the power of the government. For example, the legislative branch can only pass laws; the executive branch only carries out the laws but cannot make them; and the judicial branch determines disputes and the constitutionality of governmental actions, but cannot make laws. The power of making laws is limited by the procedure that must be followed according to Article I. In that procedure, a law does not become the law until both the House and Senate pass it and then the president approves it. Also, power is divided between the federal and state governments.

These limits help guarantee each individual's liberty from governmental interference. The Supreme Court's job is to uphold the Constitution and protect the rights and freedom of the people.

Each year the Supreme Court makes decisions which affect all aspects of American life. These decisions affect the wealthy and poor, whites, African-Americans, Hispanics, and other racial groups. They affect the way business is conducted, how children are educated, health care, criminal and monetary issues. The sample decisions and cases mentioned in this book are just a brief glimpse of how the Supreme Court has applied the Constitution.

By understanding this all-important document you take the first step toward observing and deciding for yourself if the Constitution is being upheld, or if you need to inform your elected representatives how you feel about certain issues or elect new representatives.

By studying the Constitution you know what are your rights. Just as important, you know the rights of other people. If they read the Constitution, then they know your rights as well as their own. In that shared knowledge lies the foundation of a free society and respect for others.

Please share your knowledge of the Constitution with a friend.

"I know of no safe depository of the ultimate powers of the society but the people themselves; and if we think them not enlightened enough to exercise their control with a wholesome discretion, the remedy is not to take it from them, but to inform their discretion by education. This is the true corrective of abuses of constitutional power."

—Thomas Jefferson

The Declaration of Independence: A Transcription

Note: The following text is a transcription of the Declaration of Independence in its original form.

IN CONGRESS, July 4, 1776.
The unanimous Declaration of the thirteen united States of America,

When in the Course of human events, it becomes necessary for one people to dissolve the political bands which have connected them with another, and to assume among the powers of the earth, the separate and equal station to which the Laws of Nature and of Nature's God entitle them, a decent respect to the opinions of mankind requires that they should declare the causes which impel them to the separation.

We hold these truths to be self-evident, that all men are created equal, that they are endowed by their Creator with certain unalienable Rights, that among these are Life, Liberty and the pursuit of Happiness.—That to secure these rights, Governments are instituted among Men, deriving their just powers from the consent of the governed, —That whenever any Form of Government becomes destructive of these ends, it is the Right of the People to alter or to abolish it, and to institute new Government, laying its foundation on such principles and organizing its powers in such form, as to them shall seem most likely to effect their Safety and Happiness. Prudence, indeed, will dictate that Governments long established should not be changed for light and transient causes; and accordingly all experience hath shewn, that mankind are more disposed to suffer, while evils are sufferable, than to right themselves by abolishing the forms to which they are accustomed. But when a long train of abuses and usurpations, pursuing invariably the same Object evinces a design to reduce them under absolute Despotism, it is their right, it is their duty, to throw off such Government, and to provide new Guards for their future security.—Such has been the patient sufferance of these Colonies; and such is now the necessity which constrains them to alter their former Systems of Government. The history of the present King of Great Britain is a history of repeated injuries and usurpations, all having in direct object the establishment of an absolute Tyranny over these States. To prove this, let Facts be submitted to a candid world.

He has refused his Assent to Laws, the most wholesome and necessary for the public good.

He has forbidden his Governors to pass Laws of immediate and pressing importance, unless suspended in their operation till his Assent should be obtained; and when so suspended, he has utterly neglected to attend to them.

He has refused to pass other Laws for the accommodation of large districts of people, unless those people would relinquish the right of Representation in the Legislature, a right inestimable to them and formidable to tyrants only.

He has called together legislative bodies at places unusual, uncomfortable, and distant from the depository of their public Records, for the sole purpose of fatiguing them into compliance with his measures.

He has dissolved Representative Houses repeatedly, for opposing with manly firmness his invasions on the rights of the people.

He has refused for a long time, after such dissolutions, to cause others to be elected; whereby the Legislative powers, incapable of Annihilation, have returned to the People at large for their exercise;

the State remaining in the mean time exposed to all the dangers of invasion from without, and convulsions within.

He has endeavoured to prevent the population of these States; for that purpose obstructing the Laws for Naturalization of Foreigners; refusing to pass others to encourage their migrations hither, and raising the conditions of new Appropriations of Lands.

He has obstructed the Administration of Justice, by refusing his Assent to Laws for establishing Judiciary powers.
He has made Judges dependent on his Will alone, for the tenure of their offices, and the amount and payment of their salaries.

He has erected a multitude of New Offices, and sent hither swarms of Officers to harrass our people, and eat out their substance.

He has kept among us, in times of peace, Standing Armies without the Consent of our legislatures.

He has affected to render the Military independent of and superior to the Civil power.

He has combined with others to subject us to a jurisdiction foreign to our constitution, and unacknowledged by our laws; giving his Assent to their Acts of pretended Legislation:

For Quartering large bodies of armed troops among us:

For protecting them, by a mock Trial, from punishment for any Murders which they should commit on the Inhabitants of these States:

For cutting off our Trade with all parts of the world:

For imposing Taxes on us without our Consent:

For depriving us in many cases, of the benefits of Trial by Jury:

For transporting us beyond Seas to be tried for pretended offences

For abolishing the free System of English Laws in a neighbouring Province, establishing therein an Arbitrary government, and enlarging its Boundaries so as to render it at once an example and fit instrument for introducing the same absolute rule into these Colonies:

For taking away our Charters, abolishing our most valuable Laws, and altering fundamentally the Forms of our Governments:

For suspending our own Legislatures, and declaring themselves invested with power to legislate for us in all cases whatsoever.

He has abdicated Government here, by declaring us out of his Protection and waging War against us.

He has plundered our seas, ravaged our Coasts, burnt our towns, and destroyed the lives of our people.

He is at this time transporting large Armies of foreign Mercenaries to compleat the works of death, desolation and tyranny, already begun with circumstances of Cruelty & perfidy scarcely paralleled in the most barbarous ages, and totally unworthy the Head of a civilized nation.

He has constrained our fellow Citizens taken Captive on the high Seas to bear Arms against their Country, to become the executioners of their friends and Brethren, or to fall themselves by their Hands.

He has excited domestic insurrections amongst us, and has endeavoured to bring on the inhabitants of our frontiers, the merciless Indian Savages, whose known rule of warfare, is an undistinguished destruction of all ages, sexes and conditions.

In every stage of these Oppressions We have Petitioned for Redress in the most humble terms: Our repeated Petitions have been answered only by repeated injury. A Prince whose character is thus marked by every act which may define a Tyrant, is unfit to be the ruler of a free people.

Nor have We been wanting in attentions to our Brittish brethren. We have warned them from time to time of attempts by their legislature to extend an unwarrantable jurisdiction over us. We have reminded them of the circumstances of our emigration and settlement here. We have appealed to their native justice and magnanimity, and we have conjured them by the ties of our common kindred to disavow these usurpations, which, would inevitably interrupt our connections and correspondence. They too have been deaf to the voice of justice and of consanguinity. We must, therefore, acquiesce in the necessity, which denounces our Separation, and hold them, as we hold the rest of mankind, Enemies in War, in Peace Friends.

We, therefore, the Representatives of the united States of America, in General Congress, Assembled, appealing to the Supreme Judge of the world for the rectitude of our intentions, do, in the Name, and by Authority of the good People of these Colonies, solemnly publish and declare, That these United Colonies are, and of Right ought to be Free and Independent States; that they are Absolved from all Allegiance to the British Crown, and that all political connection between them and the State of Great Britain, is and ought to be totally dissolved; and that as Free and Independent States, they have full Power to levy War, conclude Peace, contract Alliances, establish Commerce, and to do all other Acts and Things which Independent States may of right do. And for the support of this Declaration, with a firm reliance on the protection of divine Providence, we mutually pledge to each other our Lives, our Fortunes and our sacred Honor.

The 56 signatures on the Declaration appear in the positions indicated:

Column 1

Georgia:
Button Gwinnett
Lyman Hall
George Walton

Column 2

North Carolina:
William Hooper
Joseph Hewes
John Penn

South Carolina:
Edward Rutledge
Thomas Heyward, Jr.
Thomas Lynch, Jr.
Arthur Middleton

Column 3

Massachusetts:
John Hancock
Maryland:
Samuel Chase
William Paca
Thomas Stone
Charles Carroll of
Carrollton

Virginia:
George Wythe
Richard Henry Lee
Thomas Jefferson
Benjamin Harrison
Thomas Nelson, Jr.
Francis Lightfoot Lee
Carter Braxton

Column 4

Pennsylvania:
Robert Morris
Benjamin Rush
Benjamin Franklin
John Morton
George Clymer
James Smith
George Taylor
James Wilson
George Ross

Delaware:
Caesar Rodney
George Read
Thomas McKean

Column 5

New York:
William Floyd
Philip Livingston
Francis Lewis
Lewis Morris

New Jersey:
Richard Stockton
John Witherspoon
Francis Hopkinson
John Hart
Abraham Clark

Column 6

New Hampshire:
Josiah Bartlett
William Whipple

Massachusetts:
Samuel Adams
John Adams
Robert Treat Paine
Elbridge Gerry

Rhode Island:
Stephen Hopkins
William Ellery

Connecticut:
Roger Sherman
Samuel Huntington
William Williams
Oliver Wolcott

New Hampshire:
Matthew Thornton

The Constitution of the United States: A Transcription

Note: The following text is a transcription of the Constitution in its original form. Items that are underlined have since been amended or superseded by later Amendments.

We the People of the United States, in Order to form a more perfect Union, establish Justice, insure domestic Tranquility, provide for the common defence, promote the general Welfare, and secure the Blessings of Liberty to ourselves and our Posterity, do ordain and establish this Constitution for the United States of America.

Article. I.

Section. 1.

All legislative Powers herein granted shall be vested in a Congress of the United States, which shall consist of a Senate and House of Representatives.

Section. 2.

The House of Representatives shall be composed of Members chosen every second Year by the People of the several States, and the Electors in each State shall have the Qualifications requisite for Electors of the most numerous Branch of the State Legislature.

No Person shall be a Representative who shall not have attained to the Age of twenty five Years, and been seven Years a Citizen of the United States, and who shall not, when elected, be an Inhabitant of that State in which he shall be chosen.

Representatives and direct Taxes shall be apportioned among the several States which may be included within this Union, according to their respective Numbers, which shall be determined by adding to the whole Number of free Persons, including those bound to Service for a Term of Years, and excluding Indians not taxed, three fifths of all other Persons. The actual Enumeration shall be made within three Years after the first Meeting of the Congress of the United States, and within every subsequent Term of ten Years, in such Manner as they shall by Law direct. The Number of Representatives shall not exceed one for every thirty Thousand, but each State shall have at Least one Representative; and until such enumeration shall be made, the State of New Hampshire shall be entitled to chuse three, Massachusetts eight, Rhode-Island and Providence Plantations one, Connecticut five, New-York six, New Jersey four, Pennsylvania eight, Delaware one, Maryland six, Virginia ten, North Carolina five, South Carolina five, and Georgia three.

When vacancies happen in the Representation from any State, the Executive Authority thereof shall issue Writs of Election to fill such Vacancies.

The House of Representatives shall chuse their Speaker and other Officers; and shall have the sole Power of Impeachment.

Section. 3.

The Senate of the United States shall be composed of two Senators from each State, chosen by the Legislature thereof for six Years; and each Senator shall have one Vote.

Immediately after they shall be assembled in Consequence of the first Election, they shall be divided as equally as may be into three Classes. The Seats of the Senators of the first Class shall be vacated at the Expiration of the second Year, of the second Class at the Expiration of the fourth Year, and of the third Class at the Expiration of the sixth Year, so that one third may be chosen every second Year; and if Vacancies happen by Resignation, or otherwise, during the Recess of the Legislature of any State, the Executive thereof may make temporary Appointments until the next Meeting of the Legislature, which shall then fill such Vacancies.

No Person shall be a Senator who shall not have attained to the Age of thirty Years, and been nine Years a Citizen of the United States, and who shall not, when elected, be an Inhabitant of that State for which he shall be chosen.

The Vice President of the United States shall be President of the Senate, but shall have no Vote, unless they be equally divided.

The Senate shall chuse their other Officers, and also a President pro tempore, in the Absence of the Vice President, or when he shall exercise the Office of President of the United States.

The Senate shall have the sole Power to try all Impeachments. When sitting for that Purpose, they shall be on Oath or Affirmation. When the President of the United States is tried, the Chief Justice shall preside: And no Person shall be convicted without the Concurrence of two thirds of the Members present.

Judgment in Cases of Impeachment shall not extend further than to removal from Office, and disqualification to hold and enjoy any Office of honor, Trust or Profit under the United States: but the Party convicted shall nevertheless be liable and subject to Indictment, Trial, Judgment and Punishment, according to Law.

Section. 4.

The Times, Places and Manner of holding Elections for Senators and Representatives, shall be prescribed in each State by the Legislature thereof; but the Congress may at any time by Law make or alter such Regulations, except as to the Places of chusing Senators.

The Congress shall assemble at least once in every Year, and such Meeting shall <u>be on the first Monday in December</u>, unless they shall by Law appoint a different Day.

Section. 5.

Each House shall be the Judge of the Elections, Returns and Qualifications of its own Members, and a Majority of each shall constitute a Quorum to do Business; but a smaller Number may adjourn from day to day, and may be authorized to compel the Attendance of absent Members, in such Manner, and under such Penalties as each House may provide.

Each House may determine the Rules of its Proceedings, punish its Members for disorderly Behaviour, and, with the Concurrence of two thirds, expel a Member.

Each House shall keep a Journal of its Proceedings, and from time to time publish the same, excepting such Parts as may in their Judgment require Secrecy; and the Yeas and Nays of the Members of either House on any question shall, at the Desire of one fifth of those Present, be entered on the Journal.

Neither House, during the Session of Congress, shall, without the Consent of the other, adjourn for more than three days, nor to any other Place than that in which the two Houses shall be sitting.

Section. 6.

The Senators and Representatives shall receive a Compensation for their Services, to be ascertained by Law, and paid out of the Treasury of the United States. They shall in all Cases, except Treason, Felony and Breach of the Peace, be privileged from Arrest during their Attendance at the Session of their respective Houses, and in going to and returning from the same; and for any Speech or Debate in either House, they shall not be questioned in any other Place.

No Senator or Representative shall, during the Time for which he was elected, be appointed to any civil Office under the Authority of the United States, which shall have been created, or the Emoluments whereof shall have been encreased during such time; and no Person holding any Office under the United States, shall be a Member of either House during his Continuance in Office.

Section. 7.

All Bills for raising Revenue shall originate in the House of Representatives; but the Senate may propose or concur with

Amendments as on other Bills.

Every Bill which shall have passed the House of Representatives and the Senate, shall, before it become a Law, be presented to the President of the United States: If he approve he shall sign it, but if not he shall return it, with his Objections to that House in which it shall have originated, who shall enter the Objections at large on their Journal, and proceed to reconsider it. If after such Reconsideration two thirds of that House shall agree to pass the Bill, it shall be sent, together with the Objections, to the other House, by which it shall likewise be reconsidered, and if approved by two thirds of that House, it shall become a Law. But in all such Cases the Votes of both Houses shall be determined by yeas and Nays, and the Names of the Persons voting for and against the Bill shall be entered on the Journal of each House respectively. If any Bill shall not be returned by the President within ten Days (Sundays excepted) after it shall have been presented to him, the Same shall be a Law, in like Manner as if he had signed it, unless the Congress by their Adjournment prevent its Return, in which Case it shall not be a Law.

Every Order, Resolution, or Vote to which the Concurrence of the Senate and House of Representatives may be necessary (except on a question of Adjournment) shall be presented to the President of the United States; and before the Same shall take Effect, shall be approved by him, or being disapproved by him, shall be repassed by two thirds of the Senate and House of Representatives, according to the Rules and Limitations prescribed in the Case of a Bill.

Section. 8.

The Congress shall have Power To lay and collect Taxes, Duties, Imposts and Excises, to pay the Debts and provide for the common Defence and general Welfare of the United States; but all Duties, Imposts and Excises shall be uniform throughout the United States;

To borrow Money on the credit of the United States;

To regulate Commerce with foreign Nations, and among the several

States, and with the Indian Tribes;

To establish an uniform Rule of Naturalization, and uniform Laws on the subject of Bankruptcies throughout the United States;

To coin Money, regulate the Value thereof, and of foreign Coin, and fix the Standard of Weights and Measures;

To provide for the Punishment of counterfeiting the Securities and current Coin of the United States;

To establish Post Offices and post Roads;

To promote the Progress of Science and useful Arts, by securing for limited Times to Authors and Inventors the exclusive Right to their respective Writings and Discoveries;

To constitute Tribunals inferior to the supreme Court;

To define and punish Piracies and Felonies committed on the high Seas, and Offences against the Law of Nations;

To declare War, grant Letters of Marque and Reprisal, and make Rules concerning Captures on Land and Water;

To raise and support Armies, but no Appropriation of Money to that Use shall be for a longer Term than two Years;

To provide and maintain a Navy;

To make Rules for the Government and Regulation of the land and naval Forces;

To provide for calling forth the Militia to execute the Laws of the Union, suppress Insurrections and repel Invasions;

To provide for organizing, arming, and disciplining, the Militia, and for governing such Part of them as may be employed in the Service of the United States, reserving to the States respectively, the Appointment of the Officers, and the Authority of training the Militia according to the discipline prescribed by Congress;

To exercise exclusive Legislation in all Cases whatsoever, over such District (not exceeding ten Miles square) as may, by Cession of particular States, and the Acceptance of Congress, become the Seat of the Government of the United States, and to exercise like Authority over all Places purchased by the Consent of the Legislature of the State in which the Same shall be, for the Erection of Forts, Magazines, Arsenals, dock-Yards, and other needful Buildings;—And

To make all Laws which shall be necessary and proper for carrying into Execution the foregoing Powers, and all other Powers vested by this Constitution in the Government of the United States, or in any Department or Officer thereof.

Section. 9.

The Migration or Importation of such Persons as any of the States now existing shall think proper to admit, shall not be prohibited by the Congress prior to the Year one thousand eight hundred and eight, but a Tax or duty may be imposed on such Importation, not exceeding ten dollars for each Person.

The Privilege of the Writ of Habeas Corpus shall not be suspended, unless when in Cases of Rebellion or Invasion the public Safety may require it.

No Bill of Attainder or ex post facto Law shall be passed.

No Capitation, or other direct, Tax shall be laid, <u>unless in Proportion to the Census or enumeration herein before directed to be taken</u>.

No Tax or Duty shall be laid on Articles exported from any State.

No Preference shall be given by any Regulation of Commerce or Revenue to the Ports of one State over those of another; nor shall Vessels bound to, or from, one State, be obliged to enter, clear, or pay Duties in another.

No Money shall be drawn from the Treasury, but in Consequence of Appropriations made by Law; and a regular Statement and Account of the Receipts and Expenditures of all public Money shall be published from time to time.

No Title of Nobility shall be granted by the United States: And no Person holding any Office of Profit or Trust under them, shall, without the Consent of the Congress, accept of any present, Emolument, Office, or Title, of any kind whatever, from any King, Prince, or foreign State.

Section. 10.

No State shall enter into any Treaty, Alliance, or Confederation; grant Letters of Marque and Reprisal; coin Money; emit Bills of Credit; make any Thing but gold and silver Coin a Tender in Payment of Debts; pass any Bill of Attainder, ex post facto Law, or Law impairing the Obligation of Contracts, or grant any Title of Nobility.

No State shall, without the Consent of the Congress, lay any Imposts or Duties on Imports or Exports, except what may be absolutely necessary for executing it's inspection Laws: and the net Produce of all Duties and Imposts, laid by any State on Imports or Exports, shall be for the Use of the Treasury of the United States; and all such Laws shall be subject to the Revision and Controul of the Congress.

No State shall, without the Consent of Congress, lay any Duty of Tonnage, keep Troops, or Ships of War in time of Peace, enter into any Agreement or Compact with another State, or with a foreign Power, or engage in War, unless actually invaded, or in such imminent Danger as will not admit of delay.

Article. II.

Section. 1.

The executive Power shall be vested in a President of the United States of America. He shall hold his Office during the Term of four Years, and, together with the Vice President, chosen for the same Term, be elected, as follows:

Each State shall appoint, in such Manner as the Legislature thereof may direct, a Number of Electors, equal to the whole Number of Senators and Representatives to which the State may be entitled in the Congress: but no Senator or Representative, or Person holding an

Office of Trust or Profit under the United States, shall be appointed an Elector.

The Electors shall meet in their respective States, and vote by Ballot for two Persons, of whom one at least shall not be an Inhabitant of the same State with themselves. And they shall make a List of all the Persons voted for, and of the Number of Votes for each; which List they shall sign and certify, and transmit sealed to the Seat of the Government of the United States, directed to the President of the Senate. The President of the Senate shall, in the Presence of the Senate and House of Representatives, open all the Certificates, and the Votes shall then be counted. The Person having the greatest Number of Votes shall be the President, if such Number be a Majority of the whole Number of Electors appointed; and if there be more than one who have such Majority, and have an equal Number of Votes, then the House of Representatives shall immediately chuse by Ballot one of them for President; and if no Person have a Majority, then from the five highest on the List the said House shall in like Manner chuse the President. But in chusing the President, the Votes shall be taken by States, the Representation from each State having one Vote; A quorum for this purpose shall consist of a Member or Members from two thirds of the States, and a Majority of all the States shall be necessary to a Choice. In every Case, after the Choice of the President, the Person having the greatest Number of Votes of the Electors shall be the Vice President. But if there should remain two or more who have equal Votes, the Senate shall chuse from them by Ballot the Vice President.

The Congress may determine the Time of chusing the Electors, and the Day on which they shall give their Votes; which Day shall be the same throughout the United States.

No Person except a natural born Citizen, or a Citizen of the United States, at the time of the Adoption of this Constitution, shall be eligible to the Office of President; neither shall any Person be eligible to that Office who shall not have attained to the Age of thirty five Years, and been fourteen Years a Resident within the United States.

In Case of the Removal of the President from Office, or of his Death, Resignation, or Inability to discharge the Powers and Duties of the said Office, the Same shall devolve on the Vice President, and the Congress may by Law provide for the Case of Removal, Death, Resignation or Inability, both of the President and Vice President, declaring what Officer shall then act as President, and such Officer shall act accordingly, until the Disability be removed, or a President shall be elected.

The President shall, at stated Times, receive for his Services, a Compensation, which shall neither be increased nor diminished during the Period for which he shall have been elected, and he shall not receive within that Period any other Emolument from the United States, or any of them.

Before he enter on the Execution of his Office, he shall take the following Oath or Affirmation:—"I do solemnly swear (or affirm) that I will faithfully execute the Office of President of the United States, and will to the best of my Ability, preserve, protect and defend the Constitution of the United States."

Section. 2.

The President shall be Commander in Chief of the Army and Navy of the United States, and of the Militia of the several States, when called into the actual Service of the United States; he may require the Opinion, in writing, of the principal Officer in each of the executive Departments, upon any Subject relating to the Duties of their respective Offices, and he shall have Power to grant Reprieves and Pardons for Offences against the United States, except in Cases of Impeachment.

He shall have Power, by and with the Advice and Consent of the Senate, to make Treaties, provided two thirds of the Senators present concur; and he shall nominate, and by and with the Advice and Consent of the Senate, shall appoint Ambassadors, other public Ministers and Consuls, Judges of the supreme Court, and all other Officers of the United States, whose Appointments are not herein otherwise provided for, and which shall be established by Law: but the Congress may by Law vest the Appointment of such inferior Officers, as they think proper, in the President alone, in the Courts of Law, or in the Heads of Departments.

The President shall have Power to fill up all Vacancies that may happen during the Recess of the Senate, by granting Commissions which shall expire at the End of their next Session.

Section. 3.

He shall from time to time give to the Congress Information of the State of the Union, and recommend to their Consideration such Measures as he shall judge necessary and expedient; he may, on extraordinary Occasions, convene both Houses, or either of them, and in Case of Disagreement between them, with Respect to the Time of Adjournment, he may adjourn them to such Time as he shall think proper; he shall receive Ambassadors and other public Ministers; he shall take Care that the Laws be faithfully executed, and shall Commission all the Officers of the United States.

Section. 4.

The President, Vice President and all civil Officers of the United States, shall be removed from Office on Impeachment for, and Conviction of, Treason, Bribery, or other high Crimes and Misdemeanors.

Article III.

Section. 1.

The judicial Power of the United States shall be vested in one supreme Court, and in such inferior Courts as the Congress may from time to time ordain and establish. The Judges, both of the supreme and inferior Courts, shall hold their Offices during good Behaviour, and shall, at stated Times, receive for their Services a Compensation, which shall not be diminished during their Continuance in Office.

Section. 2.

The judicial Power shall extend to all Cases, in Law and Equity, arising under this Constitution, the Laws of the United States, and Treaties made, or which shall be made, under their Authority;—to all Cases affecting Ambassadors, other public Ministers and Consuls;—to all Cases of admiralty and maritime Jurisdiction;—to Controversies to which the United States shall be a Party;—to Controversies between two or more States;— between a State and Citizens of another State,—between Citizens of different States,—between Citizens of the same State claiming Lands under Grants of different States, and between a State, or the Citizens thereof, and foreign States, Citizens or Subjects.

In all Cases affecting Ambassadors, other public Ministers and Consuls, and those in which a State shall be Party, the supreme Court shall have original Jurisdiction. In all the other Cases before mentioned, the supreme Court shall have appellate Jurisdiction, both as to Law and Fact, with such Exceptions, and under such Regulations as the Congress shall make.

The Trial of all Crimes, except in Cases of Impeachment, shall be by Jury; and such Trial shall be held in the State where the said Crimes shall have been committed; but when not committed within any State, the Trial shall be at such Place or Places as the Congress may by Law have directed.

Section. 3.

Treason against the United States, shall consist only in levying War against them, or in adhering to their Enemies, giving them Aid and Comfort. No Person shall be convicted of Treason unless on the Testimony of two Witnesses to the same overt Act, or on Confession in open Court.

The Congress shall have Power to declare the Punishment of Treason, but no Attainder of Treason shall work Corruption of Blood, or Forfeiture except during the Life of the Person attainted.

Article. IV.

Section. 1.

Full Faith and Credit shall be given in each State to the public Acts, Records, and judicial Proceedings of every other State. And the Congress may by general Laws prescribe the Manner in which such Acts, Records and Proceedings shall be proved, and the Effect thereof.

Section. 2.

The Citizens of each State shall be entitled to all Privileges and Immunities of Citizens in the several States.

A Person charged in any State with Treason, Felony, or other Crime, who shall flee from Justice, and be found in another State, shall on Demand of the executive Authority of the State from which he fled, be delivered up, to be removed to the State having Jurisdiction of the Crime.

No Person held to Service or Labour in one State, under the Laws thereof, escaping into another, shall, in Consequence of any Law or Regulation therein, be discharged from such Service or Labour, but shall be delivered up on Claim of the Party to whom such Service or Labour may be due.

Section. 3.

New States may be admitted by the Congress into this Union; but no new State shall be formed or erected within the Jurisdiction of any other State; nor any State be formed by the Junction of two or more States, or Parts of States, without the Consent of the Legislatures of the States concerned as well as of the Congress.

The Congress shall have Power to dispose of and make all needful Rules and Regulations respecting the Territory or other Property belonging to the United States; and nothing in this Constitution shall be so construed as to Prejudice any Claims of the United States, or of any particular State.

Section. 4.

The United States shall guarantee to every State in this Union a Republican Form of Government, and shall protect each of them against Invasion; and on Application of the Legislature, or of the Executive (when the Legislature cannot be convened), against domestic Violence.

Article. V.

The Congress, whenever two thirds of both Houses shall deem it necessary, shall propose Amendments to this Constitution, or, on the Application of the Legislatures of two thirds of the several States, shall call a Convention for proposing Amendments, which, in either Case, shall be valid to all Intents and Purposes, as Part of this Constitution, when ratified by the Legislatures of three fourths of the several States, or by Conventions in three fourths thereof, as the one or the other Mode of Ratification may be proposed by the Congress; Provided that no Amendment which may be made prior to the Year One thousand eight hundred and eight shall in any Manner affect the first and fourth Clauses in the Ninth Section of the first Article; and that no State, without its Consent, shall be deprived of its equal Suffrage in the Senate.

Article. VI.

All Debts contracted and Engagements entered into, before the Adoption of this Constitution, shall be as valid against the United States under this Constitution, as under the Confederation.

This Constitution, and the Laws of the United States which shall be made in Pursuance thereof; and all Treaties made, or which shall be made, under the Authority of the United States, shall be the supreme Law of the Land; and the Judges in every State shall be bound thereby, any Thing in the Constitution or Laws of any State to the Contrary notwithstanding.

The Senators and Representatives before mentioned, and the Members of the several State Legislatures, and all executive and judicial Officers, both of the United States and of the several States, shall be bound by Oath or Affirmation, to support this Constitution; but no religious Test shall ever be required as a Qualification to any Office or public Trust under the United States.

Article. VII.

The Ratification of the Conventions of nine States, shall be sufficient for the Establishment of this Constitution between the States so ratifying the Same.

The Word, "the," being interlined between the seventh and eighth Lines of the first Page, the Word "Thirty" being partly written on an Erazure in the fifteenth Line of the first Page, The Words "is tried" being interlined between the thirty second and thirty third Lines of the first Page and the Word "the" being interlined between the forty third and forty fourth Lines of the second Page.

Attest William Jackson Secretary

done in Convention by the Unanimous Consent of the States present the Seventeenth Day of September in the Year of our Lord one thousand seven hundred and Eighty seven and of the Independance of the United States of America the Twelfth In witness whereof We have hereunto subscribed our Names,

G°. Washington
Presidt and deputy from Virginia

Delaware
Geo: Read
Gunning Bedford jun
John Dickinson
Richard Bassett
Jaco: Broom

Maryland
James McHenry
Dan of St Thos. Jenifer
Danl. Carroll

Virginia
John Blair
James Madison Jr.

North Carolina
Wm. Blount
Richd. Dobbs Spaight
Hu Williamson

South Carolina
J. Rutledge
Charles Cotesworth Pinckney
Charles Pinckney
Pierce Butler

Georgia
William Few
Abr Baldwin

New Hampshire
John Langdon
Nicholas Gilman

Massachusetts
Nathaniel Gorham
Rufus King

Connecticut
Wm. Saml. Johnson
Roger Sherman

New York
Alexander Hamilton

New Jersey
Wil: Livingston
David Brearley
Wm. Paterson
Jona: Dayton

Pennsylvania
B Franklin
Thomas Mifflin
Robt. Morris
Geo. Clymer
Thos. FitzSimons
Jared Ingersoll
James Wilson
Gouv Morris

Preamble to the Bill of Rights and Amendments 1 through 27: A Transcription

[The Preamble to The Bill of Rights]

Congress of the United States
begun and held at the City of New-York, on Wednesday the fourth of March, one thousand seven hundred and eighty nine.

THE Conventions of a number of the States, having at the time of their adopting the Constitution, expressed a desire, in order to prevent misconstruction or abuse of its powers, that further declaratory and restrictive clauses should be added: And as extending the ground of public confidence in the Government, will best ensure the beneficent ends of its institution.

RESOLVED by the Senate and House of Representatives of the United States of America, in Congress assembled, two thirds of both Houses concurring, that the following Articles be proposed to the Legislatures of the several States, as amendments to the Constitution of the United States, all, or any of which Articles, when ratified by three fourths of the said Legislatures, to be valid to all intents and purposes, as part of the said Constitution; viz.

ARTICLES in addition to, and Amendment of the Constitution of the United States of America, proposed by Congress, and ratified by the Legislatures of the several States, pursuant to the fifth Article of the original Constitution.

Note: The following text is a transcription of the first ten amendments to the Constitution in their original form. These amendments were ratified December 15, 1791, and form what is known as the "Bill of Rights."

Amendment I

Congress shall make no law respecting an establishment of religion, or prohibiting the free exercise thereof; or abridging the freedom of speech, or of the press; or the right of the people peaceably to assemble, and to petition the Government for a redress of grievances.

Amendment II

A well regulated Militia, being necessary to the security of a free State, the right of the people to keep and bear Arms, shall not be infringed.

Amendment III

No Soldier shall, in time of peace be quartered in any house, without the consent of the Owner, nor in time of war, but in a manner to be prescribed by law.

Amendment IV

The right of the people to be secure in their persons, houses, papers, and effects, against unreasonable searches and seizures, shall not be violated, and no Warrants shall issue, but upon probable cause, supported by Oath or affirmation, and particularly describing the place to be searched, and the persons or things to be seized.

Amendment V

No person shall be held to answer for a capital, or otherwise infamous crime, unless on a presentment or indictment of a Grand Jury, except in cases arising in the land or naval forces, or in the Militia, when in actual service in time of War or public danger; nor shall any person be subject for the same offence to be twice put in jeopardy of life or limb; nor shall be compelled in any criminal case to be a witness against himself, nor be deprived of life, liberty, or property, without due process of law; nor shall private property be taken for public use, without just compensation.

Amendment VI

In all criminal prosecutions, the accused shall enjoy the right to a speedy and public trial, by an impartial jury of the State and district wherein the crime shall have been committed, which district shall have been previously ascertained by law, and to be informed of the nature and cause of the accusation; to be confronted with the witnesses against him; to have compulsory process for obtaining witnesses in his favor, and to have the Assistance of Counsel for his defence.

Amendment VII

In Suits at common law, where the value in controversy shall exceed twenty dollars, the right of trial by jury shall be preserved, and no fact tried by a jury, shall be otherwise re-examined in any Court of the United States, than according to the rules of the common law.

Amendment VIII

Excessive bail shall not be required, nor excessive fines imposed, nor cruel and unusual punishments inflicted.

Amendment IX

The enumeration in the Constitution, of certain rights, shall not be construed to deny or disparage others retained by the people.

Amendment X

The powers not delegated to the United States by the Constitution, nor prohibited by it to the States, are reserved to the States respectively, or to the people.

AMENDMENT XI

Passed by Congress March 4, 1794. Ratified February 7, 1795.

Note: Article III, section 2, of the Constitution was modified by amendment 11.

The Judicial power of the United States shall not be construed to extend to any suit in law or equity, commenced or prosecuted against one of the United States by Citizens of another State, or by Citizens or Subjects of any Foreign State.

AMENDMENT XII

Passed by Congress December 9, 1803. Ratified June 15, 1804.

Note: A portion of Article II, section 1 of the Constitution was superseded by the 12th amendment.

The Electors shall meet in their respective states and vote by ballot for President and Vice-President, one of whom, at least, shall not be an inhabitant of the same state with themselves; they shall name in their ballots the person voted for as President, and in distinct ballots the person voted for as Vice-President, and they shall make distinct lists of all persons voted for as President, and of all persons voted for as Vice-President, and of the number of votes for each, which lists they shall sign and certify, and transmit sealed to the seat of the government of the United States, directed to the President of the Senate; — the President of the Senate shall, in the presence of the Senate and House of Representatives, open all the certificates and the votes shall then be counted; — The person having the greatest number of votes for President, shall be the President, if such number be a majority of the whole number of Electors appointed; and if no person have such majority, then from the persons having the highest numbers not exceeding three on the list of those voted for as President, the House of Representatives shall choose immediately, by ballot, the President. But in choosing the President, the votes shall be taken by states, the representation from each state having one vote; a quorum for this purpose shall consist of a member or members from two-thirds of the states, and a majority of all the states shall be necessary to a choice. [And if the House of Representatives shall not choose a President whenever the right of choice shall devolve upon them, before the fourth day of March next following, then the Vice-President shall act as President, as in case of the death or other constitutional disability of the President. —]* The person having the greatest number of votes as Vice-President, shall be the Vice-President, if such number be a majority of the whole number of Electors appointed, and if no person have a majority, then from the two highest numbers on the list, the Senate shall choose the Vice-President; a quorum for the purpose shall consist of two-thirds of the whole number of Senators, and a majority of the whole number shall be necessary to a choice. But no person constitutionally ineligible to the office of President shall be eligible to that of Vice-President of the United States.

Superseded by section 3 of the 20th amendment.

AMENDMENT XIII

Passed by Congress January 31, 1865. Ratified December 6, 1865.

Note: A portion of Article IV, section 2, of the Constitution was superseded by the 13th amendment.

Section 1.
Neither slavery nor involuntary servitude, except as a punishment for crime whereof the party shall have been duly convicted, shall exist within the United States, or any place subject to their jurisdiction.

Section 2.
Congress shall have power to enforce this article by appropriate legislation.

AMENDMENT XIV

Passed by Congress June 13, 1866. Ratified July 9, 1868.

Note: Article I, section 2, of the Constitution was modified by section 2 of the 14th amendment.

Section 1.
All persons born or naturalized in the United States, and subject to the jurisdiction thereof, are citizens of the United States and of the State wherein they reside. No State shall make or enforce any law which shall abridge the privileges or immunities of citizens of the United States; nor shall any State deprive any person of life, liberty, or property, without due process of law; nor deny to any person within its jurisdiction the equal protection of the laws.

Section 2.
Representatives shall be apportioned among the several States according to their respective numbers, counting the whole number of persons in each State, excluding Indians not taxed. But when the right to vote at any election for the choice of electors for President and Vice-President of the United States, Representatives in Congress, the Executive and Judicial officers of a State, or the members of the Legislature thereof, is denied to any of the male inhabitants of such

State, being twenty-one years of age,* and citizens of the United States, or in any way abridged, except for participation in rebellion, or other crime, the basis of representation therein shall be reduced in the proportion which the number of such male citizens shall bear to the whole number of male citizens twenty-one years of age in such State.

Section 3.

No person shall be a Senator or Representative in Congress, or elector of President and Vice-President, or hold any office, civil or military, under the United States, or under any State, who, having previously taken an oath, as a member of Congress, or as an officer of the United States, or as a member of any State legislature, or as an executive or judicial officer of any State, to support the Constitution of the United States, shall have engaged in insurrection or rebellion against the same, or given aid or comfort to the enemies thereof. But Congress may by a vote of two-thirds of each House, remove such disability.

Section 4.

The validity of the public debt of the United States, authorized by law, including debts incurred for payment of pensions and bounties for services in suppressing insurrection or rebellion, shall not be questioned. But neither the United States nor any State shall assume or pay any debt or obligation incurred in aid of insurrection or rebellion against the United States, or any claim for the loss or emancipation of any slave; but all such debts, obligations and claims shall be held illegal and void.

Section 5.

The Congress shall have the power to enforce, by appropriate legislation, the provisions of this article.

Changed by section 1 of the 26th amendment.

AMENDMENT XV

Passed by Congress February 26, 1869. Ratified February 3, 1870.

Section 1.

The right of citizens of the United States to vote shall not be denied or abridged by the United States or by any State on account of race, color, or previous condition of servitude—

Section 2.
The Congress shall have the power to enforce this article by appropriate legislation.

AMENDMENT XVI

Passed by Congress July 2, 1909. Ratified February 3, 1913.

Note: Article I, section 9, of the Constitution was modified by amendment 16.

The Congress shall have power to lay and collect taxes on incomes, from whatever source derived, without apportionment among the several States, and without regard to any census or enumeration.

AMENDMENT XVII

Passed by Congress May 13, 1912. Ratified April 8, 1913.

Note: Article I, section 3, of the Constitution was modified by the 17th amendment.

The Senate of the United States shall be composed of two Senators from each State, elected by the people thereof, for six years; and each Senator shall have one vote. The electors in each State shall have the qualifications requisite for electors of the most numerous branch of the State legislatures.

When vacancies happen in the representation of any State in the Senate, the executive authority of such State shall issue writs of election to fill such vacancies: Provided, That the legislature of any State may empower the executive thereof to make temporary appointments until the people fill the vacancies by election as the legislature may direct.

This amendment shall not be so construed as to affect the election or term of any Senator chosen before it becomes valid as part of the Constitution.

AMENDMENT XVIII

Passed by Congress December 18, 1917. Ratified January 16, 1919. Repealed by amendment 21.

Section 1.
After one year from the ratification of this article the manufacture, sale, or transportation of intoxicating liquors within, the importation thereof into, or the exportation thereof from the United States and all territory subject to the jurisdiction thereof for beverage purposes is hereby prohibited.

Section 2.
The Congress and the several States shall have concurrent power to enforce this article by appropriate legislation.

Section 3.
This article shall be inoperative unless it shall have been ratified as an amendment to the Constitution by the legislatures of the several States, as provided in the Constitution, within seven years from the date of the submission hereof to the States by the Congress.

AMENDMENT XIX

Passed by Congress June 4, 1919. Ratified August 18, 1920.

The right of citizens of the United States to vote shall not be denied or abridged by the United States or by any State on account of sex.

Congress shall have power to enforce this article by appropriate legislation.

AMENDMENT XX

Passed by Congress March 2, 1932. Ratified January 23, 1933.

Note: Article I, section 4, of the Constitution was modified by section 2 of this amendment. In addition, a portion of the 12th amendment was superseded by section 3.

Section 1.
The terms of the President and the Vice President shall end at noon on

the 20th day of January, and the terms of Senators and Representatives at noon on the 3d day of January, of the years in which such terms would have ended if this article had not been ratified; and the terms of their successors shall then begin.

Section 2.
The Congress shall assemble at least once in every year, and such meeting shall begin at noon on the 3d day of January, unless they shall by law appoint a different day.

Section 3.
If, at the time fixed for the beginning of the term of the President, the President elect shall have died, the Vice President elect shall become President. If a President shall not have been chosen before the time fixed for the beginning of his term, or if the President elect shall have failed to qualify, then the Vice President elect shall act as President until a President shall have qualified; and the Congress may by law provide for the case wherein neither a President elect nor a Vice President shall have qualified, declaring who shall then act as President, or the manner in which one who is to act shall be selected, and such person shall act accordingly until a President or Vice President shall have qualified.

Section 4.
The Congress may by law provide for the case of the death of any of the persons from whom the House of Representatives may choose a President whenever the right of choice shall have devolved upon them, and for the case of the death of any of the persons from whom the Senate may choose a Vice President whenever the right of choice shall have devolved upon them.

Section 5.
Sections 1 and 2 shall take effect on the 15th day of October following the ratification of this article.

Section 6.
This article shall be inoperative unless it shall have been ratified as an amendment to the Constitution by the legislatures of three-fourths of the several States within seven years from the date of its submission.

AMENDMENT XXI

Passed by Congress February 20, 1933. Ratified December 5, 1933.

Section 1.
The eighteenth article of amendment to the Constitution of the United States is hereby repealed.

Section 2.
The transportation or importation into any State, Territory, or Possession of the United States for delivery or use therein of intoxicating liquors, in violation of the laws thereof, is hereby prohibited.

Section 3.
This article shall be inoperative unless it shall have been ratified as an amendment to the Constitution by conventions in the several States, as provided in the Constitution, within seven years from the date of the submission hereof to the States by the Congress.

AMENDMENT XXII

Passed by Congress March 21, 1947. Ratified February 27, 1951.

Section 1.
No person shall be elected to the office of the President more than twice, and no person who has held the office of President, or acted as President, for more than two years of a term to which some other person was elected President shall be elected to the office of President more than once. But this Article shall not apply to any person holding the office of President when this Article was proposed by Congress, and shall not prevent any person who may be holding the office of President, or acting as President, during the term within which this Article becomes operative from holding the office of President or acting as President during the remainder of such term.

Section 2.
This article shall be inoperative unless it shall have been ratified as an amendment to the Constitution by the legislatures of three-fourths of the several States within seven years from the date of its submission to the States by the Congress.

AMENDMENT XXIII

Passed by Congress June 16, 1960. Ratified March 29, 1961.

Section 1.
The District constituting the seat of Government of the United States shall appoint in such manner as Congress may direct:

A number of electors of President and Vice President equal to the whole number of Senators and Representatives in Congress to which the District would be entitled if it were a State, but in no event more than the least populous State; they shall be in addition to those appointed by the States, but they shall be considered, for the purposes of the election of President and Vice President, to be electors appointed by a State; and they shall meet in the District and perform such duties as provided by the twelfth article of amendment.

Section 2.
The Congress shall have power to enforce this article by appropriate legislation.

AMENDMENT XXIV

Passed by Congress August 27, 1962. Ratified January 23, 1964.

Section 1.
The right of citizens of the United States to vote in any primary or other election for President or Vice President, for electors for President or Vice President, or for Senator or Representative in Congress, shall not be denied or abridged by the United States or any State by reason of failure to pay poll tax or other tax.

Section 2.
The Congress shall have power to enforce this article by appropriate legislation.

AMENDMENT XXV

Passed by Congress July 6, 1965. Ratified February 10, 1967.

Note: Article II, section 1, of the Constitution was affected by the 25th amendment.

Section 1.
In case of the removal of the President from office or of his death or resignation, the Vice President shall become President.

Section 2.
Whenever there is a vacancy in the office of the Vice President, the President shall nominate a Vice President who shall take office upon confirmation by a majority vote of both Houses of Congress.

Section 3.
Whenever the President transmits to the President pro tempore of the Senate and the Speaker of the House of Representatives his written declaration that he is unable to discharge the powers and duties of his office, and until he transmits to them a written declaration to the contrary, such powers and duties shall be discharged by the Vice President as Acting President.

Section 4.
Whenever the Vice President and a majority of either the principal officers of the executive departments or of such other body as Congress may by law provide, transmit to the President pro tempore of the Senate and the Speaker of the House of Representatives their written declaration that the President is unable to discharge the powers and duties of his office, the Vice President shall immediately assume the powers and duties of the office as Acting President.

Thereafter, when the President transmits to the President pro tempore of the Senate and the Speaker of the House of Representatives his written declaration that no inability exists, he shall resume the powers and duties of his office unless the Vice President and a majority of either the principal officers of the executive department or of such other body as Congress may by law provide, transmit within four days to the President pro tempore of the Senate and the Speaker of the House of Representatives their written declaration that the President is unable to discharge the powers and duties of his office. Thereupon Congress shall decide the issue, assembling within forty-eight hours for that purpose if not in session. If the Congress, within twenty-one days after receipt of the latter written declaration, or, if Congress is not in session, within twenty-one days after Congress is required to assemble, determines by two-thirds vote of both Houses that the President is unable to discharge the powers and duties of his office, the Vice President shall continue to discharge the same as Acting President; otherwise, the President shall resume the powers and duties of his office.

AMENDMENT XXVI

Passed by Congress March 23, 1971. Ratified July 1, 1971.

Note: Amendment 14, section 2, of the Constitution was modified by section 1 of the 26th amendment.

Section 1.
The right of citizens of the United States, who are eighteen years of age or older, to vote shall not be denied or abridged by the United States or by any State on account of age.

Section 2.
The Congress shall have power to enforce this article by appropriate legislation.

AMENDMENT XXVII

Originally proposed Sept. 25, 1789. Ratified May 7, 1992.

No law, varying the compensation for the services of the Senators and Representatives, shall take effect, until an election of representatives shall have intervened.

Glossary

This glossary defines words and special terms *as they are used in the Constitution and Declaration of Independence.* Often these are not the same definitions that are most common today. The first time a word appears in the book it is defined within the text, usually in brackets like [this]. Other definitions of these words can be found in a regular dictionary .

Abdicated: gave up a right, responsibility or duty

Abridging: reducing or restricting

Absolved: set free or released

Accommodation: the process of adapting or adjusting to someone or something

Acquiesce: agree without protest

Adhering: being attached as a follower

Adjourn: postpone action of a convened legislative body until another time specified

Admiralty and maritime jurisdiction: maritime—related to the sea or sailing—and admiralty jurisdiction covers things done upon and relating to the sea, lakes and rivers. These include transactions relating to commerce and navigation, as well as damages and injuries. Formerly these laws were administered by admirals, which explains their name.

Admit: allow

Affected: to seek to obtain; to aim at; aspire to

Affirmation: a formal legal declaration by a person who declines to take an oath for reasons of conscience (compare to *oath*)

Allegiance: tie or obligation of a person to his king or government

Ambassador: a government official of the highest rank sent by one nation to live in another nation as its representative

Annihilation: being wiped out completely

Appeal: 1) to make a request to a higher court asking that a case be reheard or reviewed; 2) to make an urgent request

Appellate: relating to appeals, which are reviews of lower court decisions by a higher court

Application: formal request to an authority; the act of making such a request

Apportioned: divided and allocated

Appropriation: 1) money set aside for a particular use; 2) assigning for a particular use

Arbitrary: 1) not based on a known reason or rule; at the whim of someone else, such as a tyrant; 2) absolute or unrestricted

Arsenals: places for making or storing weapons and other munitions.

Article: a section or part of a written document such as a constitution, treaty or contract

Ascertained: established

Assent: agreement or consent

Assume: to take

At large: 1) in general; 2) in complete detail or fully

Attainder: the loss of a person's civil rights and property because he has been sentenced to death or outlawed

Attained: reached

Attainted: punished by attainder

Bail: money given to allow the temporary release of a person from jail and to guarantee the person will return at a certain date. If the person fails to return, the money is given up.

Bands: things that bind or unite

Beneficent: causing good to be done

Bill: 1) a proposed law presented for discussion and approval; 2) a list of items. The *Bill* of Rights lists 10 basic rights.

Bill of Attainder: a law passed against a person, pronouncing him guilty, without trial, of an alleged crime (especially treason) and punishing him by death and depriving him of his civil rights and his property

Bill of credit: paper money

Blessings: benefits

Bounties: rewards offered to people by the government for performing certain acts. During the Civil War, a cash bounty was offered to men for enlisting in the army.

Brethren: people closely united or associated

Britain: "Britain" and "Great Britain" mean the island where England, Scotland and Wales are located, and since 1707 also refers to the political union of England, Scotland and Wales

Breach: violation

Candid: free from prejudice; fair or impartial

Capital: punishable by death

Capitation: a tax, fee, or charge of the same amount for every person

Cases: matters to be decided (in a court of law)

Certificates: declarations made in writing and signed by the person and intended to verify a fact

Certify: make a declaration in writing

Cession: the action of transferring the title or ownership of something to another owner

Charter: a document which outlines the conditions under which a colony is organized

Chief justice: the senior judge of the Supreme Court

Civil: 1) relating to a person as a member of a community. It comes from a Latin word meaning "city."; 2) relating to the community, or to the policy and government of the citizens

Civil liberty: the liberty of persons in a society. Society restrains "natural liberty" for the safety of its citizens. So "liberty" in a civilized society has as part of its definition the control of the individual to the extent that the individual may not harm or hinder the liberty of another individual. Unnecessary restraint of natural liberty when an individual's actions do not threaten the public good is oppression and therefore not liberty. See also *natural liberty* and *liberty*.

Colony: 1) a group of people who settle in a place away from their native land, but remain under the political control of their native land; 2) the land settled by these people.

Commander in chief: supreme commander of the armed forces

Commission: 1) a written document given to a person authorizing him to perform certain duties; 2) the act of giving a commission to a person

Common law: that body of rules, principles and customs which have been received from our ancestors, and recognized by courts. It is different from "statutory law," which is laws made by legislatures. It applies to disputes between private parties in non-criminal matters. The phrase "at common law" means according to common law.

Compact: contract or treaty

Compulsory process: a legal document ordering a person to appear in court

Conclude: to make a final determination

Concur: agree

Concurrence: agreement

Concurrent: existing at the same time

Confederation: a group of independent nations or states joined together. The Confederation was the word that referred to the United States before the Constitution was adopted.

Congress: 1) a body of persons with the power to make laws. The U.S. Congress is composed of the Senate and House of Representatives.; 2) a meeting of individuals who will deal with matters for their common good

Conjured: asked earnestly

Consanguinity: relationship by descent from the same ancestor; relationship by blood; kinship; close relationship

Consent: permission

Constellation: a group of stars that form a recognizable pattern

Constituting: forming

Constitution: 1) an agreement that sets in place a system of fundamental principles for the government of rational and social beings; 2) a system of fundamental rules, principles and laws that establishes the form of government in a state or country; 3) a document in which these fundamental laws and principles are written; 4) the state of being; or the way a thing is composed or made up

The word comes from "constitute," which means to fix or establish. So, our Constitution fixes or establishes what our government is and what it does.

Constrains: forces or compels

Construed: interpreted or explained

Consul: a person appointed by his government to live in a foreign country and serve his own country's business interests, and citizens in that foreign country

Controversies: lawsuits

Convene: to cause to assemble

Convention: meeting of delegates or representatives for consultation on important issues

Correspondence: communication

Corruption of blood: a blood relative or family member of a person guilty of treason is held guilty of his or her relative's treason. In times prior to this, sometimes a traitor's family members were also punished.

Credit: 1) confidence which people place in the ability of a nation, company or individual to repay borrowed money; 2) a reliance on the truth of something said or done

Creed: set of beliefs or aims that guide someone's actions

Crown: the power of a king

Decent: fit or suitable

Declaration: a public announcement. Declaration comes from a Latin word meaning "make quite clear."

Declare: to state that a person or thing exists in a certain way

Deem: conclude

Democracy: a government run directly by the people. "Demos," a Greek word for "the people", combined with "cracy," a Greek word meaning "to rule," to form democracy. A small town could have a democracy where each person voted on all matters concerning the town, but with millions of people in the United States, it was considered much more practical to have a "republican" form of government where the people vote for representatives who then vote on their behalf.

Denounces: announces

Deny: refuse to recognize

Depository: a place where anything is kept for safekeeping

Design: plan or purpose

Despotism: a tyranny; or unjust and oppressive government

Devolve: pass to a body or person at a lower level (said of duties and responsibilities)

Direct tax: a tax placed on a person or organization. Examples of direct taxes would be income taxes and property taxes where persons or organizations are taxed. An "indirect tax," on the other hand, taxes goods or services. Sales taxes are an example of an indirect tax.

Disavow: repudiate or condemn

Discipline: education and instruction

Disparage: regard as being of little worth

Dispose of: to deal with conclusively, or settle

Disposed: made willing; inclined

Distinct: separate

District: an area of a country or city

Domestic: refers to one's own country

Due process of law: the regular administration or course of the law

Duty: 1) a payment due to the government, especially a tax imposed on imports, exports, or manufactured goods; 2) that which a person owes to another; that which a person is bound by any natural or moral obligation to do or perform

Effect: produce or cause

Effects: personal belongings

Either: one or the other

Elector: someone who elects: a) a qualified voter or b) a person who votes at the Electoral College for president and vice president

Electoral College: "college" means an organized group with particular aims, duties and privileges. "Electoral" means relating to elections or electors. The term "Electoral College" designates the group of people that elects the president and vice president

Emancipation: the action of freeing from slavery

Emit: issue formally and with authority; put into circulation (*emit* currency)

Emolument: the gain from employment or position; payment received for work; salary, wages, fees, etc.

Ends: intended purposes

Engagements: obligations by agreement or contract

Enjoy: have, possess and use with satisfaction

Endowed: provided with a quality or power

Entangling: involving in difficulties or complicated circumstances that are difficult to get out of

Enumeration: establishing the number of something

Equity: fairness or justice. Equity is a system of rules that supplements and replaces laws in the United States when such laws are inadequate for fair settlement. It is based on principles of reason and fairness that allow the law to be adjusted to special circumstances. Originally, courts of equity were different from courts of law. Today, most states have combined the equity and law courts into one court system.

Establish: set up on a permanent basis

Evinces: shows or indicates

Ex Post Facto: after the fact. An *ex post facto* law is one which applies to actions committed before the law was passed. Taken from a Latin phrase meaning "from a thing done afterward."

Excise: a tax on the manufacture, sale, or consumption of various commodities within a country, such as liquor, tobacco, etc.

Excited: created (He has *excited* domestic insurrections)

Execution: the putting into operation

Executive: refers to the branch of government that administers laws and government affairs

Executive departments: currently there are fifteen executive departments, such as the Departments of Defense, Commerce and Agriculture. The principal officers of these departments are called secretaries and, along with the vice president, make up the president's "cabinet" or group of advisors.

Exercise: performance of duties

Expedient: proper under the circumstances

Faith: belief; confidence; trust

Fatiguing: weaken by harassing

Federal: the system of national government that deals with matters that individual states have in common (even though the individual states have their own state governments) is called the "federal system." The federal government is also called the national government, the government of the United States, or the central government.

The word "federal" comes from a Latin word, which means "league." "League" means an alliance between states for their mutual aid and defense; a national agreement. A key element is their agreement. "Federal" means a league of states that have agreed to cooperate with each other for a specific purpose or purposes. Hence, we have our federal government of the United States, which is the central or national government. This federal government is made from the agreement of the states to cooperate with each other.

Felony: a major crime such as murder, arson, rape, etc.

Fit: convenient

Forfeiture: a giving up of something as a penalty, such as losing one's property as a payment for a crime

Formidable: feared or dreaded

Free: able to think or act without restriction; independent

Free person: someone who is not a slave

General: concerning all or most people

Government: 1) the action of controlling or regulating a nation; 2) the fundamental system by which a country is ruled

The word "government" comes from "govern," which means to direct or control the actions and conduct of men, either by established laws or by the will of the ruler.

Grand jury: a grand jury is a jury that investigates allegations of a crime and issues indictments if it finds there is sufficient evidence against the person or persons

Ground: foundation; that which supports anything

Habeas corpus: Latin for "you are ordered to have the body." A writ of habeas corpus is a legal document ordering a person to be brought before a court; specifically, an order requiring that a detained person be brought before a court at a stated time and place to decide the legality of his detention or imprisonment.

Happiness: that agreeable state of being in which desires are gratified; the enjoyment of pleasure without pain; good fortune. It comes from a root meaning "chance" and "good fortune." So the right to the "pursuit [from the Latin 'follow forward'] of happiness" contains the idea that you are free to follow a path that leads to good fortune—whatever goal that represents for you.

Herein: in this document

High crimes: great or punishable by death

High seas: the open ocean not under the jurisdiction of a country

Hither: to this place

House: a group of people elected to make laws. It is part of the legislative branch of government. Congress is made up of two separate branches called "houses." One house is named the House of Representatives, with its members usually called "representatives"; the other house is the Senate and its members are called "senators."

Humble: submissive

Immunities: freedoms

Impeachment: charging the holder of a public office with misconduct. Under the Constitution, the House of Representatives makes a written charge against an official (the impeachment) and then, after impeachment, the Senate sits as a court, hears evidence and gives a verdict.

Impel: drive or urge forward

Impost: a tax, especially a tax on imported goods

In consequence: as a result

In general: relating to or including all members

Indictment: a formal written charge against one or more people presented to a court

Inestimable: too valuable or precious to be properly measured or estimated

Inevitably: unavoidably

Infamous crime: one which is punishable by imprisonment or death

Inferior officers: government officials of lower rank than ambassadors, Supreme Court judges, etc.

Instituted: established

Instrument: someone or something used as a means for accomplishing a specific purpose

Insurrections: violent uprising against authority or government

Invested: provided with something

Involuntary servitude: a slave-like condition. Sometimes British criminals were sold to American colonists to labor for them during the term of their sentence.

Judicial: refers to judges, courts or their functions

Judiciary: dealing with courts of law

Junction: act of joining

Jurisdiction: 1) the power to make, declare or apply the law; 2) the power to govern

Just: honest; conforming to moral and proper principles of social conduct

Justice: 1) behavior or treatment based on what is morally right or fair; 2) the administration of the law or authority in maintaining this; 3) a judge on the Supreme Court

Kindred: relationship by blood

Laid: imposed a burden or penalty

Law: rules established by governments for regulating people's actions.

Law of nations: rules that regulate dealings between nations coming from principles of justice, customs or agreements between nations

Laws of Nature: nature is the entire universe; or the creator of all things or the operation of the power that creates all things. The Laws of Nature include the idea of unchanging moral principles that form the basis for human conduct.

Lay: to set or impose (to *lay* and collect taxes)

Legislative: the power to make laws

Legislature: a group of persons given the power and responsibility to make laws for a country or state. The

Parliament in Great Britain and the federal Congress in the United States are both legislatures.

Letters of Marque and Reprisal: government documents authorizing an individual to arm a ship and capture enemy merchant ships and cargo. Letters of marque and reprisal are no longer used.

Levying: making (*levying* war)

Liberty: 1) free from the arbitrary [based on random choice or personal whim] control of others; 2) release or freedom from slavery, imprisonment or other restrictions. It comes from a root word meaning "belonging to the people, free" and also "to grow up, rise." See also *natural liberty, civil liberty*

Life: the condition in which a plant's, an animal's or a human being's natural functions and motions are performed. In humankind, that state of being in which the spirit, intellect and body are united we identify as life. The source of the word "life" goes back to a meaning of "to be." So when we say "life" we are speaking about our right to be and to regulate or conduct our own existence.

Magazines: places of storage or military supply depots

Magnanimity: the quality of being noble and generous in one's conduct and rising above pettiness or meanness

Majority: more than half

Manly: brave

Measures: 1) inches, feet, yards, acres, etc.; 2) actions to be taken

Mercenaries: hired soldiers

Militia: body of soldiers organized from the civilian population in times of emergencies. When they are not needed for military duties, they pursue their usual occupations.

Misconstruction: mistaking the true meaning

Misdemeanors: offenses less serious than crimes

Mock: imitating reality but not real

Mode: manner; method

Native: produced by nature; natural

Natural liberty: the power to act as one thinks fit without any restraint or control except from the laws of nature

Naturalization: giving to a person of foreign birth the rights of citizenship in a new country

Nay: a "no" vote

Net: remaining from an amount of money after all deductions have been made

Notwithstanding: without being affected by the particular factor mentioned

Oath: a formal declaration with an appeal to God for the truth of what is being declared

Object: aim or goal

Office: a particular duty or employment

Officers: 1) people appointed to positions of authority in a government; 2) people appointed to positions of rank and authority in the armed services

Ordain: officially order

Original jurisdiction: the authority to try a case from its beginning

Other officers: people appointed to positions of responsibility in the government

Other public ministers: government officials representing their own government in another country and ranking below an ambassador

Overt act: "overt" means open or public. An "overt act" is a legal term meaning an actual open and outward action taken to further a crime. For example, thinking about pulling out a gun and robbing someone would not be an overt act, but actually pulling out a gun and robbing someone would be.

Pardon: lessening or setting aside the punishment for a crime

Parliament: a group of people that make the laws for a country

Paralleled: equaled

Peace: that quiet, order and security which is guaranteed by the laws

People: the group of persons who make up a nation

Perfidy: treachery

Persuasion: belief

Petitioned: made a formal request

Political: relating to government or public affairs

Poll tax: 1) a tax per "head"; 2) a tax on each person collected before they may vote. The old English meaning of "poll" was a person's "head."

Post roads: roads over which mail is carried

Posterity: all of a person's descendants; all future generations or future mankind

Powers: 1) influential countries; 2) rights or authorities

Prejudice: to injure, or harm because of some action

Prescribe: order or direct

Presentment: a report made by a grand jury of an offense that the grand jury observed or learned during their investigations

President pro tempore: a senator who presides over the U.S. Senate in the absence of the vice president. The vice president of the United States is the official presiding officer of the Senate, but in modern times generally presides over the Senate only on ceremonial occasions or when a tie-breaking vote is needed.

Primary election: a state election to choose candidates for public office. The word "primary" means first. These elections are followed by the election where the final choice is made.

Privileged: exempted

Pro tempore: temporary

Probable cause: a valid reason in presuming someone is guilty of some illegal act

Produce: that which is yielded

Provide: 1) make available for use; 2) make adequate preparation; enable or allow

Provided: "provided" is used in legal documents to introduce a condition or requirement

Providence: God or the protective care of nature as a spiritual power

Prudence: good judgment

Public: in open view

Publish: formally announce

Pursuance: the carrying out of something in the way that is expected or required

Quartering: lodging

Quorum: the minimum number of members of an assembly required to be present to make the actions of that assembly valid

Ratify: to give formal approval to something

Recess: suspension of business

Rectitude: correctness of behavior

Redress: the setting right of what is wrong; satisfaction or compensation for a wrong or injury

Reformation: the correction of anything corrupt

Render: cause to be; make

Representative houses: legislatures. They are composed of representatives of the people who meet and make laws. The House of Lords and the House of Commons in Great Britain and the Senate and the House of Representatives in the United States are representative houses.

Reprieves: postponements of punishments

Republic: a form of government in which supreme power rests with all the people and their elected representatives, and which has an elected president rather than a king or queen

Requisite: required or necessary

Reserving: retaining

Resolution: formal statement of opinion or intention by a legislature

Respect: 1) that positive view or honor in which we hold the good qualities of others; 2) in view of; considering, regarding

Respecting: regarding

Respectively: separately or individually

Returns: reports on the count of votes at polling places

Rhode Island and Providence Plantations: the name of four early settlements in what is now Rhode Island

Right: 1) a power or privilege which correctly belongs to one by law, nature or tradition; 2) *verb* to relieve from wrong; restore to normal or correct condition; 3) *of right* as a result of having a moral or legal claim

Seat: 1) location or site; Washington, D.C. is the *seat* of the national government; 2) a place in an elected legislature or other body

Secure: to make certain, to make safe, to guard effectively from danger

Securities: IOUs, such as savings bonds issued by the U.S. government

Self-evident: producing certainty or clear conviction upon direct observation

Several: individual, separate or distinct. The several states would be the separate, individual states, such as New York, Virginia, Georgia, etc.

Sitting: engaged in its business

Speaker: the officer presiding over a lawmaking body, such as the House of Representatives

Standing: remaining permanently in existence

Station: position or rank

Subscribed: signed at the end of a document

Substance: means of living

Sufferable: able to be tolerated

Sufferance: tolerance; endurance, such as of pain or misery

Suffrage: the right to vote

Tenure: the duration, act, manner, or right of holding something, such as an elected office or other position

Thereby: by or through that

Therefore: for that reason

Therein: in that place

Thereof: of that

Train: a series

Tranquility: calmness

Transient: short duration; not lasting

Treatise: a written work dealing formally and systematically with a subject

Tribunals: courts

Try: examine according to law, as in a court

Tyranny: oppressive or unjust government

Unalienable: not capable of being sold, separated or transferred to another

Undistinguished: not making a distinction among or between

Union: 1) a group of independent states joined together for some specific purpose; 2) the United States of America

Unwarrantable: unjustified

Usurpation: the wrongful or forceful taking of a right or power

Vest: place in the control of a person or group

Viz: a contraction of a Latin word meaning "that is to say"

Wanting: lacking

Weights: ounces, pounds, etc.

Welfare: prosperity and happiness

Whatsoever: of any kind

Works: actions, deeds, achievements

Writ: a formal legal document ordering some action

Writs of election: formal written documents ordering elections

Writ of Habeas Corpus: see habeas corpus

Yea: a "yes" vote

Bibliography

These are some of the books and materials that inspired and educated me as I set out to learn about the Constitution and guided me in writing this book. The original handwritten Constitution, the Bill of Rights and the Declaration of Independence are on display at the National Archives and are worthy of a visit if you are ever in Washington, D.C.

American Dictionary Of The English Language—Noah Webster. 1828 edition. Reprinted by the Foundation for American Christian Publishers. 1967, 1995.

Common Sense—Thomas Paine, edited with an Introduction by Isaac Kramnick. Penguin Books. 1776, 1986.

The Constitution of the United States, An Introduction— Floyd G. Cullop. Mentor, an imprint of New American Library, a division of Penguin Books USA Inc. 1984.

The Encyclopaedia Britannica—The Encyclopaedia Britannica Company. 11th edition. 1911.

Frederick Douglass and the Fourth of July—James A. Colaiaco. Palgrave Macmillan. 2006.

The Making of America, The Substance and Meaning of the Constitution—W. Cleon Skousen. The National Center for Constitution Studies. 1985.

The National Archives Experience—The National Archives. www.archives.gov/national-archives-experience/visit/visit.html

The National Constitution Center www.constitutioncenter.org

A Postulate Out Of A Golden Age—L. Ron Hubbard (A lecture recorded on 6 December 1956). Golden Era Productions. 2004. Distributed by Bridge Publications.

The World Book Encyclopedia—World Book-Childcraft International, Inc., Chicago. 1979.

Index

Page numbers in **bold** refer to the original documents. Page numbers in *italic* refer to information in sidebars or illustrations.

Prohibition of alcohol, 62, 116, 118, 146–147

repeal of, 150

Property, seizure of, 61, 92–93, 95, 110, 128

Property tax, 69–71

Puerto Rico, 114

Punishment, cruel and unusual, 61, 129–130

Pursuit of happiness, right to, 7, 9, 32

Q

Quebec, 40–41

R

Rebellion of farmers, 48

Religion, freedom of, 60, 173

Representation, right of, 35

Representation based on population, 49–50, 68–69, 140–141

Representatives. *See* House of Representatives

Republicans (political party), 133–134

Republics (governments), 12–13, 16, 114–115

Revolution, American. *See* American Revolution

Revolutionary War. *See* American Revolution

Right of assembly, 60, 124–125, 173

Right of representation, 35

Right to bear arms, 60, 125–126

Right to due process of law, 91–92

Right to elect government, 33

Right to fair trial, 61, 108–109, 127–129

Right to liberty, 8, 32

Right to life, 7–8, 32

Right to petition government, 60, 124–125

Right to pursuit of happiness, 7, 9, 32

Right to vote, 16, 62–63, 140–141, 143, 147, 161–162

Rights, general, 7, 17, 61, 130–131

W

About the Author

The People's Guide To The United States Constitution was inspired by a 1992 Presidential debate. The three Presidential candidates seemed to contradict each other on Constitutional issues and the author was shocked to realize that, even with his background as the Legal Director of a U.S. based international software firm, he was not familiar enough with the Constitution to determine which candidates, if any, were telling the truth.

Being the independent type, Dave Kluge did not want some politician's or scholar's interpretation of these issues, so he set out to read the original text and clarify for himself the framers' intent. Yet many hours later, up to his elbows in dictionaries, encyclopedias and other texts, it became clear that, while the well-educated framers made conscientious efforts to communicate exactly what they meant, some of the original meanings of the words they used over two centuries ago have been lost to modern dictionaries. The effort that it took to source key words of the articles of the Constitution and research their historical context in order to come to his own understanding, made Dave wonder how the average working man or woman could find time to do the same.

Writing without political bias, Dave has penned *The People's Guide to the United States Constitution* with the simple goal of helping today's Americans to easily read the Constitution in its original form and thereby achieve a true understanding without the aid of interpretations.

Dave now promotes broader understanding of the Constitution through his study guides for educators and self-study, and his blog on Constitutional basics which can be read at **understandtheconstitution.com**.